God's Guide for Grandparents

GOD'S
Guide
for
Grandparents

Susan M. Erschen

**Our
Sunday
Visitor**

www.osv.com
Our Sunday Visitor Publishing Division
Our Sunday Visitor, Inc.
Huntington, Indiana 46750

Copyright © 2017 by Susan M. Erschen. Published 2017.

22 21 20 19 18 17   1 2 3 4 5 6 7 8 9

All rights reserved. With the exception of short excerpts for critical reviews, no part of this work may be reproduced or transmitted in any form or by any means whatsoever without permission from the publisher. For more information, visit: www.osv.com/permissions.

Our Sunday Visitor Publishing Division
Our Sunday Visitor, Inc.
200 Noll Plaza
Huntington, IN 46750
1-800-348-2440

ISBN: 978-1-68192-100-6 (Inventory No. T1835)
eISBN: 978-1-68192-152-5
LCCN: 2017947642

Cover design: Amanda Falk
Cover art: Shutterstock
Interior design: M. Urgo

PRINTED IN THE UNITED STATES OF AMERICA

ABOUT THE AUTHOR

Susan Erschen writes frequently on the spirituality of giving, gratitude, living simply, and spending time with God. Her articles have appeared in *America, The Priest* magazine, *Our Sunday Visitor, St. Anthony Messenger*, and *Today's Catholic Teacher*. She is the former Director of Stewardship Education for the Archdiocese of St. Louis. She enjoys spending time with family and volunteering in her parish community.

For my dear grandchildren, with love always

CONTENTS

Introduction

The front door opened at my sister's house and the lilting voice of her daughter could be heard calling out, "Guess who's coming to Grandma's house?"

My sister just beamed as her daughter carried her three-week-old grandson into the room. "I just love that my house is now 'Grandma's House,'" my sister said. "Do you ever get tired of hearing that?" she asked me.

"No," I smiled, "you never get tired of it." Little fingerprints now appear mysteriously on all my windows and mirrors. A collection of sippy cups sits on a kitchen shelf that once held wine glasses. The front of my refrigerator is decorated with scribbled drawings. And my desk drawers are full of "I ♥ U Grandma" notes crafted in crayon. Yes, I am thrilled I now live in a place called, by some very dear children, "Grandma's House."

Being a grandparent is truly one of life's greatest blessings. It is the fulfillment of Scripture's beautiful prayer, "May you … / … live to see your children's children" (Ps 128:5–6). These words are a part of many wedding liturgies. We may not give them much thought when we are on the threshold of the next stage of our lives. However, when the child we once cradled in our arms hands us his or her own child to hold for the first time, a cosmic shift occurs in our lives. We may never be the same again. With God's guidance and grace the change can hopefully be a joyful and beautiful one.

We may not even remember all we thought about when we held our first grandchild. It can be a time of great emotion — joy mixed with worry. We may have wondered where the years went. How we could possibly be old enough to be a grandparent? We may have been counting fingers and toes and asking for assurances that everyone was well. We surely marveled at the beauty of this new life and wondered who the baby looked like. One thing I do remember most vividly as I held my first granddaughter was thinking how could I possibly be worthy of this precious little girl God had sent into my life. How could I be a good grandmother to her? How could I give her all the love and support, the memories and lessons she would need from me for life in a world very different from the one into which I had been born?

THE GIFT OF A GRANDCHILD

A grandchild is certainly an amazing gift. The little one may carry 25 percent of our genetic code. Even in cases where adoption or stepparents may be part of the family history, a grandchild is a wonderful and new chapter in our story. More importantly, this child comes directly to us from the hands of God. It has been many years since we grandparents were children ourselves. Maybe we have lost some of our wonder along the way, or forgotten God's loving touch. Maybe we have developed bad habits or failed in some way to be all God intended us to be. Grandchildren, however, can introduce us anew to God's goodness.

Grandchildren invite us to a new youthfulness. We might worry that being a grandparent makes us old. Certainly, we will feel new aches and pains as we begin again to rock an infant to sleep, chase after a toddler, or grab a little one from harm's way. But grandchildren also give us a second chance to live life with renewed hope, contentment, gratitude, awe, love, and joy.

Of course, some grandparent experiences are not all giggles, hugs, and joy. Some grandchildren arrive at inconvenient times. Some are ill. Some may be with us for too short a time. Some arrive in alienated or dysfunctional families. Some grandparents and grandchildren get to spend little or no time together. Yet, even in these saddest and most difficult cases, a grandchild can have a profound impact on our lives. Grandchildren — even ones we may never get to meet — can leave a lasting mark on our hearts.

An old legend says the indentation on a baby's upper lip, right below the nose, is a mark left by God. Before God sends a child into the world, he gently places his finger on that spot to seal into our memories all the love, peace, and joy of the Divine. It is why, when we want to remember something, we may place a finger on this little ridge. The one thing we all long to remember is what God is like. Above everything else, grandchildren can remind us of that.

THE ROLE OF A GRANDPARENT

Precisely because a grandchild may renew our faith in the glory of God, we have a joyful obligation to introduce our grandchildren to this wonderful God. But we do not have the ultimate responsibility. Almost every grandparent says one of the blessings of being a grandparent is not being responsible for raising this new generation of children. That primary responsibility belongs to the parents. We have tackled that tough job already, and we know it is demanding, exhausting, and frustrating. But it is also the most rewarding job in the world. And now our sons and daughters are embracing it. Where does that leave us?

We still have an important role to play. In fact, it may be the last big role we play in life. From the moment of our birth, we all play many roles. We start out as sons or daughters, siblings, grandchildren ourselves, possibly also nieces and nephews. We become friends, spouses, parents, employees, bosses, volunteers, and neighbors. But the last and greatest role we may play is that of a grandparent. This is a role from which we will never retire. It is not a starring role. It is only a supporting role — one in which we support the parents in their critical work of raising our beautiful and precious grandchildren. Yet, if we play this role well, we can have a lasting impression on the lives of our grandchildren. We can impart to them valuable faith lessons and introduce them to the joy, grace, and peace our faith can give us. Let us ask God every day to help us play this last role well.

In *The Joy of Love,* Pope Francis notes the significance of this role: "Very often it is grandparents who ensure that the most important values are passed down to their grandchildren, and 'many people can testify that they owe their initiation into the Christian life to their grandparents.' Their words, their affection, or simply their presence help children to realize that history did not begin with them, that they are now part of an age-old pilgrimage and that they need to respect all that came before them" (*Amoris Laetitia,* 192).

The wisdom of grandparents has always been critical to the survival of the family. Many anthropologists believe that thousands of years ago it was the grandparents' knowledge which helped humanity survive. The older ones knew where to find water in times of drought or where to find food in times of famine. Today, our families do not need us to find food and water for them. However, they do need us to support them in other ways. This overbusy, over-stressed world places great demands on young families. Each family will need support from grandparents in different ways. At the very least, we can help prepare our grandchildren to carry Christ into a world which will be very different from the one we know — a world of new technologies, new challenges, and new fears.

Modern media lets us stay connected to our grandchildren no matter how far away they are from us. One woman has a Sunday afternoon story time with her faraway grandchildren. She reads library books to them over Skype every weekend. One little boy calls his grandmother "Grandma in the Box," because they spend so much time together on Skype. One of my friends phones her out-of-town grandchildren every evening to say a quick "good night" and hear one thing about their day. Her son says the kids look forward to that call all day. They carefully plan what they want to tell Grandma. Staying in touch with our grandchildren is important. It sets the stage for letting us share our faith and spirituality with them.

FAITH AND SPIRITUALITY

If we want to pass our faith onto our grandchildren, we first need to take a close look at what we have to offer them. Today's children expect everything to do something. By the time they are a year old, our grandchildren know what brightly colored buttons to push on all their toys to make them sing, dance, wiggle, or giggle. If a toy doesn't do something, a child quickly becomes bored with it. Sadly, the same can be said of our faith.

Faith, quite simply, is what we believe. Spirituality is what we do with our faith. If we set our faith up on a shelf, point to it, and tell our grandchildren, "This is what you must believe," it will inspire them little more than a toy with a dead battery. But if they see us living those beliefs, then we are giving them something of value.

We cannot hope to teach our grandchildren the faith merely by reading them a children's book of Bible stories published thirty years ago. While those stories are beautiful, today's grandchildren need to know how faith works right now. The way we live the Gospel in our lives — and especially in our interaction with them and their families — will teach our grandchildren the values they will need for a Spirit-filled future.

We cannot give, however, what we ourselves do not have. If our faith, virtues, and spirituality are meager, we cannot expect to pass them on in abundance to our grandchildren. At this grandparenting stage of our lives, it might be time to dust off our own approach to the Faith and give it a fresh look. We might want to spruce up our spirituality or make sure our virtues are sparkling. This could be the greatest gift we will give our grandchildren. Let us make sure it is the best it can be.

In his Second Letter to the Corinthians, Saint Paul wrote, "You are our letter, written on our hearts, known and read by all" (3:2). The apostle was referring to the fact that other people would consider the value of this new faith based on what they saw in the Corinthians. This has not changed in two thousand years. Years from now, future generations will be judging the value of the same faith Paul preached based on what they see in our grandchildren. We have an opportunity to let our faith be known by how our grandchildren see it lived in us.

Do we have the kind of spirituality necessary to inspire faith in our grandchildren? We certainly must make sure our spiritual batteries are freshly charged. We may go to Mass on Sundays and even pray a Rosary now and then, but is our faith truly vibrant? Do our lives sparkle with compassion and generosity? Is our acceptance of all people a catchy tune our grandchildren will want to sing? Do they see service shining through our lives? Is our respect for nature and all of God's creation a joyful dance they want to follow? Do our grandchildren see us as loving, kind, and generous — not just to them, but to all those we encounter throughout our lives? Do we glow with trust, peace, hope, joy, and contentment? Do we walk in God's mercy, showing forgiveness to others in the same way God forgives our own weaknesses?

These are the Gospel values and the teachings of today's Church which we must pass on to our grandchildren. These are the standards by which they will consciously or unconsciously judge the faith of their grandparents and decide whether it has value and strength for them and the future they face.

The virtues we are called to share with our grandchildren are not necessarily prized by our secular world. The world will teach our grandchildren about assertiveness, power, attractiveness, and prestige. We can teach them God's lessons. These are the virtues taught to us by the Father in the Old Testament, the Son in the Gospels, and the Holy Spirit through the writings of the apostles and other saints.

As a young seminarian, Pope John XXIII wrote in his journal, "I am good at thinking up virtues, not at practicing them" (*Journal of a Soul*). That can certainly be said of me. It can probably be said of all of us. As grandparents, we have one more chance to practice what we preach. We can show a new generation how to live with virtue. As we have throughout our lives, we will surely fail at times. But let us admit it promptly when we do and never stop trying.

We are never too old to deepen and enrich our own faith life. We are never too old to study sacred Scripture in a new way, to read the wise writings of saints and popes, to embrace a deeper expression of our faith or to practice living the Gospel more fully. There is always another step for us to take on our faith journey. Like the smallest mustard seed, even a little effort to enliven our faith now can make a huge difference in the faith of our grandchildren. We need to improve and expand our own spirituality so it will be a strong-enough witness for our grandchildren, who will face secular, materialistic, and social challenges to their faith much stronger than anything we have faced. Every grandparent wants to give his or her grandchild the best they can give. The best we have to offer is not some material possession or some wild adventure. The best we have to give is our relationship with God and how we live trusting in him.

We cannot guarantee a safe and bountiful future for our grandchildren. Yet, we can do much to help them be spiritually prepared to face whatever blessings or challenges their lives may bring.

Our children may curiously observe us doing things for our grandchildren that we never did for them. Wouldn't it be great if one of the things we could do for our grandchildren was live our faith better than we have ever done before? Let us try our best. We owe it to our grandchildren.

Chapter 1

Obedience

It is 3:00 a.m. My grandchildren are spending the night at our house. My one-year-old grandson is sleeping peacefully in his crib. My three-year-old granddaughter is standing by the side of my bed, telling me she is still afraid to go to sleep. She has been awake for two hours now. I have tried everything. I have taken her back to her bed, assuring her we have no monsters in our house. I have lain on the floor by her bed, hoping she would not be afraid if I was there. I have let her climb into my bed, but she thought it was a grand time for whispered talk. We have played soft music, turned on an extra light, read three books by flashlight, and had more drinks of water than I could count. I even turned on a movie, hoping she would fall asleep to that. But now the movie is over and she is still awake and wanting to go downstairs and play with toys.

I explain to her — for the hundredth time — it is still nighttime and not playtime. I am reduced to begging. I plead with her to just go back to bed, close her eyes, and sleep.

"Grandma," she replies with all sincerity, "I would really like to help you out, but I just don't like sleeping."

THE WISDOM OF OUR CHILDREN

"I would really like to help you out, but ..." I have heard my son use those same words in response to my granddaughter's whining for something he had told her she could not have. He and his wife both have a gentle but consistent way of letting the kids know they cannot always have what they want. I am extremely proud of the way they are raising their children. Yet, intentionally or unintentionally, we grandparents can sometimes get in the way of the parenting work our children are doing. We may fail to honor their wishes and obey their rules. This can be harmful to our grandchildren.

Because I attended a Jesuit university, I was required to take nine credit hours of theology. I took World Religions, Scriptures, and Theology of Marriage. Those courses had a big impact on my life. I remember the Theology of Marriage professor saying the best thing parents can do for their children is to love their spouse. Every child needs to feel his or her parents are good, wise, and lovable. If children see their parents as bad or wrong, they often tend to think something is wrong with them, too. They know they are closely connected to their parents. So, when we criticize, undermine, or contradict our grandchildren's parents, we take a little piece away from our grandchildren's sense of worth. This is not good. Grandparents should interfere in the raising of a grandchild only in the most extreme cases in which the welfare of the child is at risk.

Pope Francis emphasizes the importance of letting parents be right when he says: "It is irresponsible to disparage the other parent as a means of winning a child's affection or out of revenge or self-justification. Doing so will affect the child's interior tranquility and cause wounds hard to heal" (*The Joy of Love*, 245). If this is the pope's advice for parents, it certainly would apply to grandparents, too. For the sake of the children, we must honor their parents in every way possible.

This may not always be easy. Our children's marriages are not without challenges. The people they marry might bring with them different family traditions, expectations, worldviews, and beliefs. We must accept whatever the situation might be.

Young parents today work hard to do the best for their children. In this era of information overload, they sort through endless dos and don'ts. Their pediatricians give them lots of rules. Their friends give them advice. If they check the Internet, they quickly are overwhelmed with information "every parent should know." Long gone are the days when you just referred to the index in Dr. Spock's baby book or called your mom. Once our children sort through all this information, we must respect the rules they set down. Every young family has the right to set its own rules, just as we once set the rules for our own families. Although the new parents make the rules, they still want our support. A December 2015 Pew study found 72 percent of young parents hope their parents approve of the way they raise their children. Let us give them that approval and support.

A good example comes from a grandmother who spent an afternoon entertaining her infant granddaughter with soothing baby videos she found on YouTube. When the parents came home she was proud to tell them of this great discovery. The young parents were not thrilled. They gently told Grandma they did not want their baby exposed to electronic media until she was at least a year old. Grandma did as all good grandparents should do. She immediately apologized and promised to respect their wishes in the future.

Modern technology presents many new issues for parents and grandparents to discuss. Can grandparents post pictures of grandchildren or announce family events on their Facebook page? What kind of television shows, movies, and video games do the parents find acceptable? Should grandparents send out a photo Christmas card of their grandchildren? When is it okay for Grandma or Grandpa to text, phone, FaceTime, or Skype a grandchild? These and similar questions should be discussed — always mindful and respectful of the fact that the parents should make the rules, not the grandparents.

Sometimes the rules young parents set down may not make sense to us. We are still called to respect them. Think of the ten lepers who were cured by Jesus (see Lk 17:11–19). The lepers asked to be cured. Jesus replied, "Go show yourselves to the priests" (v. 14). This command surely made no sense to the lepers. They could have argued. But instead they did as they were asked. Scripture tells us, "As they were going they were cleansed." It was only when they obeyed Our Lord's instructions that they were cured. If they would have stood around arguing with Jesus, they may never have been cured. Let us not argue when we are asked to do something (or refrain from doing something), even if it does not make sense to us. In fact, even if we strongly disagree.

Best practices in child-care have changed so much in the last generation that some hospitals now offer classes for new grandparents. If I would have taken one of those classes, maybe I would not have been shocked when my daughter-in-law fixed a bottle for my baby granddaughter with powdered formula and tap water from a public restroom. Sterilizing bottles is out. Swaddling babies is in. Regardless of the new rules, God calls us to honor and obey the parents in all things. No one knows the child better than they. In this way, we can help our grandchildren learn to obey their parents, their heavenly Father, and other authority figures in their lives.

THE WILL OF THE FATHER

God gave Moses the Ten Commandments. The first three cover our relationship with God. The next seven cover our relationship with others. The first of the human-relations commandments is, "Honor your father and your mother, that you may have a long life in the land the LORD your God is giving you" (Ex 20:12). Teaching our grandchildren this commandment is the perfect way to start passing our faith onto them. However, it will not be enough to just tell them, "Do what your mommy and daddy tell you." We, too, must do what their mommy and daddy wish. Giving our grandchildren the idea it is okay to disobey is not okay at all.

Obedience is a virtue we usually think applies only to children and vowed religious. However, the Church says this commandment calls all of us to respect and obey all those in authority. We must be faithful Christians, law-abiding citizens, and good employees. If we do this, we generally have the Fourth Commandment covered. Except, now, there is a new sheriff in town. Our children — the parents of our grandchildren — are in authority over our grandchildren. That means they are in authority over us and our relationship with our grandchildren. We must honor and respect them. We cannot respond to their wishes with an "I'd really like to help you out, but …" attitude.

In his Letter to the Romans, Saint Paul tells us why obedience is necessary: "Let every person be subordinate to the higher authorities, for there is no authority except from God, and those that exist have been established by God. Therefore, whoever resists authority opposes what God has appointed, and those who oppose it will bring judgment upon themselves" (13:1–2). The authority God has established over our grandchildren is their parents. It is not us! According to Paul, if we decide to oppose that authority, we are opposing God.

Young parents make their rules based on new research and information. This is good. This is progress. It has been that way since the beginning of time. At the end of the creation story we are told, "A man leaves his father and mother and clings to his wife, and the two of them become one body" (Gn 2:24). Jesus reinforced this teaching,: "Have you not read that from the beginning the Creator 'made them male and female' and said, 'For this reason a man shall leave his father and mother and be joined to his wife, and the two shall become one flesh'? So, they are no longer two, but one flesh. Therefore, what God has joined together, no human being must separate" (Mt 19:4–6). We must not separate young parents by questioning the decisions they have made about parenting their children. We can give advice if — and only if — we are asked.

Pope Francis stresses the control God has entrusted to parents by teaching, "God allows parents to choose the name by which he himself will call their child for all eternity" (*The Joy of Love*, 166). If God, as the Creator, so completely respects the wishes of a parent, then surely we, as the grandparents, must do the same.

OBEDIENCE IN THE GOSPELS

The life of Jesus is a model of obedience for us. Mary was obedient to the wishes of God by agreeing to be the mother of his Son. As far as we know, her parents, Saint Anne and Saint Joachim, were not consulted in the matter. God did not send an angel to see if Anne and Joachim approved of Mary's "yes." Because of a decision entirely out of their control, Saints Joachim and Anne became the grandparents of Jesus and the patron saints of grandparents for all ages. Their feast day is July 26.

Jesus, too, lived the virtue of obedience. After Jesus was lost in the Temple, "He went down with them and came to Nazareth, and was obedient to them; and his mother kept all these things in her heart" (Lk 2:51). If Christ, the Lord, can be obedient to his human parents, surely we can honor the wishes of our grandchildren's parents.

Obedience is a virtue we see throughout the Gospels. At the wedding at Cana we see Jesus honor his mother's wish that he intervene. More importantly, we hear the Blessed Mother tell us to obey. Mary speaks very rarely in Scripture. But her few words to the servers at the Cana feast are words for all of us: "Do whatever he tells you" (Jn 2:5). These words are the preface to every teaching and every command Jesus will utter in his public life. They are spoken to us, who are servants to God, as much as they were spoken to the servants at the wedding feast.

In her "Prayer for Acquiring Humility," Saint Thérèse of Lisieux reflected on the many ways Jesus was obedient in his life and even today. Not only was he obedient to his parents, but he was obedient to those who tried, tortured, and killed him. And today he is obedient to every priest who utters the words of consecration at the altar. Saint Thérèse wrote: "At their word, you come down from heaven. Whether they advance or delay the hour of the Holy Sacrifice, you are always ready."

His agony in the garden shows us that Jesus himself struggled with all it meant to obey the Father completely. Yet, he trusted in God and followed his will. If we are agonizing over decisions our grandchildren's parents might be making, we can kneel with Jesus in the Garden of Gethsemane and pray with all our hearts for God to change the situation. But we must not interfere.

THE POWER OF THE SPIRIT

Keeping infants away from computer screens is certainly not an agonizing rule to follow. However, it can be heartbreaking when the parents refuse to bring their children to the sacraments or to talk to them about God. As difficult as it can be, these are still wishes we must respect. Sadly, many grandparents destroy their relationships with children and grandchildren over such issues. Some have even tried to have their grandchildren secretly baptized. When we do this we are undermining the authority of our grandchildren's parents and showing our total lack of trust in the grace of God and the workings of the Holy Spirit.

God gives children the graces they will need. Remember, he loves them even more than we do! Sacraments are powerful and wonderful signs of God working in our lives. Seeing a grandchild baptized or receiving holy Communion for the first time can bring a grandparent to tears of joy. However, God will still be in the life of a child who does not receive the sacraments. He will give them the grace they need. Remember, he loves them. The God who knocked Saul to the ground and converted him from killing Christians to being one of the greatest Christian leaders can surely touch the hearts and souls of our grandchildren. The sacraments of the Church are beautiful gifts through which God works in our lives. But God does not need them. We are the ones who need them.

Pope Francis warns us, "To raise doubts about the working of the Spirit, to give the impression that it cannot take place in those who are not 'part of our group,' who are not 'like us,' is a dangerous temptation" (Apostolic Journey to Philadelphia, September 27, 2015). To stress his point the pontiff quoted Jesus: "If you then, who are wicked, know how to give good gifts to your children, how much more will the Father in heaven give the holy Spirit to those who ask him?" (Lk 11:13).

So, let us pray to God to bless our grandchildren with the graces of the Holy Spirit. Let us pray to the Holy Spirit to guide young parents and lead them and their children to the graces he longs to give them through the sacraments of the Church. Let us ask Our Lord to help us respect and honor the parents of our grandchildren, so we can humbly accompany them on their sacred journey to raise our grandchildren.

For Reflection

1. What parenting decisions and techniques used by my grandchildren's parents most impress me? Do I let

these young parents know of my support for the good work they are doing in raising their children?

2. What can I do to help my grandchildren see that I respect and honor their parents?

3. Do I fully respect the right of my sons and daughters — both those by birth and by marriage — to make the rules and raise their children as they think best? If not, why not?

4. Do I believe God loves my grandchildren even better than I do? Do I trust he can overcome any obstacle in bringing these children into relationship with him?

A Grandparent's Prayer

Heavenly Father, you have commanded us to honor fathers and mothers. Help me to honor and respect the parents of my grandchildren. Let me never do anything to undermine the authority you have given them over their children. Help me to model for my grandchildren how to be obedient to the wishes of those in authority over them. I bow humbly to you and to all those you have trusted with authority. Amen.

Chapter 2

Acceptance

"I can't wait until I am a grandparent," a friend once said to me.

"Don't wish your life away," I told him. He was a young man with five children under the age of ten. I was a grandmother enjoying my first grandchild. Why would he want to fast forward his life to the stage where I was?

He was an outstanding dad. He cherished his time with his young children. Yet, he explained why he also envied my position. He told me I had more of the fun and good times and less of the difficult and tough moments. He was right.

A comic bumper sticker says, "Grandchildren are your reward for not killing your children." While being a parent is a wonderfully joyful and rewarding experience, being a grandparent is somehow just a little better. Being a parent is like climbing beautiful mountains. But it also comes with the risk of being plunged down into deep and dark valleys. Being a grandparent is like being on a plateau of joy. Parents have a profound love and pride for their children, but they also know worry, frustration, and impatience. We grandparents often have a more level relationship with our grandchildren.

In a homily on the feast of Saints Joachim and Anne, the patron saints of grandparents, our parish priest said, "I have never met a grandparent who did not think his or her grandchildren were the most perfect, amazing grandchildren ever." It is true that as grandparents we get to see more of the good in our grandchildren and less of the naughty. We have more fun times with them and less of the work and discipline. We are able to enjoy their strengths and their goodness, while parents have to deal with their weaknesses and faults.

THE ACCEPTANCE OF YOUTH

So, what can we learn from all this goodness we see in our grandchildren. One virtue I admire in my young grandchildren is acceptance. It seems to me they are very accepting of people and situations that we adults may have learned to judge in negative ways.

When my granddaughter was only three years old, her family moved to a new home thirty minutes from her preschool. Even though it meant driving over an hour a day just to take her to or from her old preschool, her parents made the decision to let her finish out the semester there. They did not want her to experience too much turmoil in her life all at once. She loved everything about that preschool. She loved her teachers. She loved the playground. She loved all her friends. I worried how she would adapt to being put into a new school after the Christmas break.

As grandparents often do, I worried unnecessarily. The first time I saw her after she had started in the new school she was bubbling over with enthusiasm for her new school, her new teachers, and her new friends. I admired the acceptance with which she embraced the change in her life. She especially talked about her new friend. He was so funny. He made her laugh. He was so nice. He showed her where everything was in her new classroom. He helped her when she was confused because they did things differently in this new school. He smiled at her when she was nervous or afraid. What she did not tell me — because she never even noticed — was that her new friend was of a racial background different from hers and he wore special glasses for a vision problem. None of this registered with her. She accepted him and liked him completely for the person he was inside. I thought how wonderful our world would be if we all were as accepting as this three-year-old.

Unfortunately, we rarely make use of the opportunity to learn from children. Instead, we tend to teach them our bad habits. This point was made in the musical *South Pacific*. Ahead of its times, the Richard Rodgers and Oscar Hammerstein production that premiered in 1949 and was made into a film in 1958 explored the tension and sadness prejudice can cause in our lives. One of the songs in the show is "You've Got to Be Carefully Taught." It suggests that very small children do not pay attention to the differences in people. Yet, sometime around grade-school age, kids start mimicking the prejudices they see in the adults around them. Racism is something we learn as children, something we are, as the song says, "carefully taught." We are not born with prejudices.

Prejudices are nothing new. The world into which Jesus was born was full of prejudices. The Jews did not like the Samaritans. The Romans hated the Jews. Even the apostle Bartholomew, originally known as Nathanael, had prejudices. When his friend Phillip told him about Jesus, Nathanael said to him, "Can anything good come from Nazareth?" (Jn 1:46).

Yet, Jesus ignored and broke through all prejudices. The story of his birth shows the infant welcoming two groups not accepted in Judea — shepherds and foreigners. Throughout his life, he embraced those who were generally not accepted — lepers, Samaritans, tax collectors, and women. We are called to do the same. For the sake of our grandchildren, let us try to let go of the prejudices we may hold. The world will be a better place if we do.

SEEING JESUS IN OTHERS

To overcome our prejudices, however, we need to become aware of them. Only then can we avoid passing these biases to our grandchildren. Young children are often blind to the differences they see in others. Maybe that is one of the reasons why Our Lord told us, "Amen, I say to you, whoever does not accept the kingdom of God like a child will not enter it" (Lk 18:17). In this area, let us strive to be more like our grandchildren, rather than teaching them to be like us!

Let's admit it: Many of us love to judge. We all do it sometimes. We judge whether an outfit looks good on someone. We judge whether a home is neat and attractive. We judge whether children are well-behaved. We judge the quality of the produce we buy for dinner, the data in a report we are reviewing, the value of an item compared to the cost we must pay. We might say judging is important because it helps us make good decisions.

The problem, Saint Paul tells us, is when we judge other people. He admits, "Indeed, I wish everyone to be as I am, but each has a particular gift from God, one of one kind and one of another" (1 Cor 7:7). As Christians we are called to accept the differences between us and the unique qualities that belong to each of us. We are asked to see others (and ourselves) as God sees them. We are told that it is possible to see Jesus in every person because he lives in each one of us.

I don't know about you, but I am not very good at seeing Jesus in others. I have never turned around and seen Jesus pushing his cart too close to me in a checkout line. I have never seen Jesus driving the car that just cut me off. I have never seen Jesus instead of the woman who is blowing cigarette smoke my way as we pass on the sidewalk. All I see are human faces that belong to people who at the moment are annoying me and making it difficult for me to accept rather than judge. Although I am not good at seeing Jesus in others, I have had some success imagining Jesus with other people.

We can begin by imagining Jesus with our grandchildren. We can imagine Jesus running with them to the playground, sitting with them building blocks, or laying with them on a pile of pillows watching television. Once we have gotten used to seeing Jesus with our grandchildren we can try imaging Jesus with someone we might be judging.

My first attempt at this strategy brought me to laughter. An older man, whom I had judged to be arrogant and foolish, roared past me on the road in a convertible sports car that screamed midlife crisis. I tried to imagine Jesus with this man, sitting in the passenger seat with him. Jesus was not berating him for his bad investment. Instead, Our Lord had his arm over the back of the seat, laughing with his long hair blowing out behind him in the breeze. That helped me realize how totally wrong I was to judge this man and his situation.

Pope Francis tells us, "It is a profound spiritual experience to contemplate our loved ones with the eyes of God and to see Christ in them" (*The Joy of Love*, 323). Seeing Christ with them may not be quite as profound, but it can be an easier place to start.

WHAT WE DO NOT KNOW

Another way to work at being more accepting of people for the benefit of our grandchildren is to consider what we do not know. We really cannot judge anyone, because we never know what their situation might be. We do not know what obstacles they have overcome just to get where they are, even if we feel they are not at a place we would consider desirable or even respectable. We never know what pain or tragedy another person is carrying.

I remember thinking this very strongly on the hot August day when we were heading to my grandfather's funeral. I had been very blessed. I had reached my midtwenties before I ever encountered significant loss, had to be part of a funeral procession, or had to walk across parched ground to a place where an open grave waited. But on the day of my grandfather's funeral I was experiencing all of this. It was miserably hot, and I was overwhelmed with the realization that my childhood was truly over as one of the first persons who had known me since the day I was born was laid to rest.

But no one else on the streets seemed to care about my heavy heart. For them it was just another hot and muggy day. They rushed past me without a moment's notice, not noticing my pain at all. I never forgot that feeling of no one knowing or caring. From time to time I still wonder how often I've caused someone else to feel that way? How often do I judge someone who is grieving, who has just received bad news, who is unemployed, or who is fighting cancer? We don't know any of those things about the people we encounter as we go about our busy lives. All we concentrate on is whether they annoy us, get in our way, or do not meet our standards of behavior or appearance. Imagine what a wonderful future it could be if each of us taught our grandchildren to be more sensitive to the burdens and concerns other people might be carrying.

Pope Francis tells us, in the document that announced the Year of Mercy to be held in 2016, why our insensitivity to the unknown burdens and struggles of others must stop: "To refrain from judgment and condemnation means, in a positive sense, to know how to accept the good in every person and to spare him any suffering that might be caused by our partial judgment, our presumption to know everything about him" (*The Face of Mercy*, 14).

OUR TOUGH STANDARDS

Consciously or unconsciously many of us judge ourselves by the same high standards that we impose on others. Even worse, some of us may expect others to live by standards we ourselves do not even meet. Either way, judging can be as harmful to ourselves as to others. That is why Jesus says, "Stop judging and you will not be judged" (Lk 6:37). If we are constantly judging others for their out-of-date clothes, old car, bad haircut, boring vacation, or unattractive houses, we must work very hard to make sure our own wardrobe, transportation, image, travel, and home all measure up to the standards we use to judge others.

Some of us also tend to judge others by their religious traditions or practices — and think that only our beliefs and practices are acceptable to God. What a great disservice we do to God when we judge him to have a heart no more merciful or accepting than ours! It reminds me of an experience I had with my eighteen-month-old granddaughter. She had come to be very fond of me. When I came into the room, she would run to me as fast as she could. She loved to have me carry her or hold her. One day she was playing contentedly on the floor when her older brother fell and hurt himself. He came running to me crying and I wrapped my arms around him and began to comfort him. My little granddaughter jumped up from where she was playing, ran to him, put both of her little hands on his chest and pushed him away from me as hard as she could, nestling herself into the place where he had been in my arms. It was as if she were saying, "My grandma and my grandma *only*." This jealous and childish behavior is much like what we do when our judgments push others away from God's love and care. We are saying, "My God and my God only."

Jesus does not judge us by our standards. Neither do our grandchildren. In their innocent love for us, our grandchildren teach us a nonjudgmental kind of acceptance and love. They do not care if we are old, have aches and pains, or wear glasses. We came into their lives after many years of journeying through this world. They accept us exactly as we are now. We do not have to pretend to be anyone different for them. That is one of the many things that makes our time with them so special.

We can help our grandchildren become more — rather than less — accepting by modeling that ourselves. When we are more willing to accept the way we are, we will become more willing to accept the way other people are. When we learn to appreciate the good in ourselves, we will learn to see the good in others. Conversely, when we learn to appreciate the good in others, we will be more likely to see the good in ourselves. This accepting attitude will make us more grateful, generous, and joyful.

When we are quick to judge others and hold them to high standards, usually we are likewise hard on ourselves. We often put more time and energy into trying to live up to society's standards than we do in trying to live up to Gospel standards. Is this the life we really want for our grandchildren? Or can we learn and teach them a different way? Can we encourage them to accept themselves and all other people as God made them to be? When we do this, we can stop expecting perfection from ourselves and others. We can relax and enjoy life so much more.

It is, of course, important to recognize that accepting others — despite the flaws and weaknesses we all have — is not the same as condoning inappropriate or immoral behavior. A dear friend is grandmother to four children whose mother abandoned them because of drug abuse. This grandmother encourages her grandchildren to still love and pray for their mother even while teaching them to avoid the mistakes their mother has made in life. Saint Timothy offers us good advice for handling such difficult situations: "First of all, then, I ask that supplications, prayers, petitions, and thanksgivings be offered for everyone. This is good and pleasing to God our savior, who wills everyone to be saved and to come to knowledge of the truth" (1 Tm 2:1,3–4). If God wants to save everyone, surely he does not want us to condemn others. Rather, let us teach our grandchildren to accept and pray for those who do wrong.

SPEAK OF THE GOOD

Sadly, our society today seems to have a hunger to hear the negative. Has the media trained us to like bad news? Or do they bombard us with it all day because they know that is what will keep us glued to our screens? We may not be able to control the headlines, but we can control our own conversations — especially around our grandchildren. Let us start paying attention to how many conversations are filled with criticism and judgment rather than praise and kind words. We may find that we don't often talk about the beautiful flowers tenderly cultivated in one person's yard but will surely discuss the junk and clutter in another's.

Saints, I believe, knew how to speak of the good. We often call a person a saint who never complains or never criticizes another person. Saint Ignatius Loyola tells us that thinking and speaking the good is a virtue we should strive to live: "Every good Christian ought to be more eager to put a good interpretation on a neighbor's statement than to condemn it" (*Spiritual Exercises*, 22).

We may think we have the freedom to say whatever we want about another person, as long as it is true. However, revealing negative information about someone — even if it is the truth — is also a form of gossip. No one needs to know another's secrets or weaknesses. Such hurtful conversations are "a sinful violation of the privacy of others" (*United States Catholic Catechism for Adults*, 434).

Even worse is to slander another person by making statements which are wrong or an exaggeration of the truth. As grandparents, we need to be alert to this kind of talk from our grandchildren. They may love to tell us stories about their friends, teachers, or siblings. If the stories seem to have a particularly negative tone, we may want to gently ask them if this is really the truth or the way it happened. We may have an opportunity to nip a bad habit in the bud.

It is much easier for us to accept one another if we look for the good rather than what is not. Our world very much needs people to see and accept the good in others. In their innocence, our grandchildren can teach us that when we forget this. In our wisdom, we can teach them when they forget. The message of the Gospel is one of acceptance. The teachings of the Church call us to love and accept one another. Aware that our grandchildren are watching us in all we say and do, let us learn to speak of the good in all people.

For Reflection

1. Do I affirm my grandchildren when they are open and accepting of others, or do I encourage them to embrace my own prejudices?

2. If my grandchildren speak negatively of another, do I help them think about why that person might appear in a negative way at that particular time? Do I encourage my grandchildren to remember that Jesus loves everyone unconditionally?

3. Do I impose materialistic and secular standards of excellence on myself or others? Is there a Gospel standard I can choose to uphold instead?

4. Do I find my conversations are often filled with judgment and negative comments? How can I learn to speak more of the good in life and less about the things I judge to be lacking?

A Grandparent's Prayer

Ever-present Spirit, please be with me always. Enter my heart when I fail to accept another one of God's children and remind me that our Father loves us all. Enable me to give up my bad habits of judging others. Help me show my grandchildren how to be loving, sensitive, and accepting of all people. I ask this through Christ our Lord, who has called me to love and accept all people. Amen.

Chapter 3

Compassion

We were laying on our bellies under the Christmas tree. Our heads brushed the lower branches of the tree and our faces were close together as we inspected the manger scene. We were discussing each figure. Mary, the mother. The shepherd, who brought a baby lamb. The angel who came to adore the new baby. Then my two-year-old grandson touched the tiny figure of Jesus with his tiny, bare arms and legs stretching out from the straw-filled crib. My grandson said, "He cold."

I wasn't sure I understood him, so I asked him to tell me again. Grabbing the soft polka-dot blanket he always had beside him, my grandson said: "He cold. Need blanket."

I clarified: "You think baby Jesus is cold and needs a blanket?"

My grandson nodded enthusiastically, popping his thumb in his mouth and rubbing his own blanket against his face.

I was amazed. This little boy, who was just learning to talk, felt compassion for a ceramic figure of Jesus.

I could have told him that the real Jesus was fine. Jesus was warm in heaven with his daddy. Yet, I knew all across our city on this cold December day Jesus really *was* cold. I did not want to discourage my grandson's budding compassion. For years, my four children made a soft bed for baby Jesus every Advent by adding pieces of gold yarn to a wooden crib when they did something nice for someone else. And every Christmas morning we carried the statue, wrapped only in its ceramic swaddling, down to the manger and placed it there before any presents could be opened. Yet never once did any of them worry if the little figure of Jesus was cold. We never wrapped the small statue in a piece of cloth. But here was my grandson full of concern for the tiny image of Jesus.

"Should we make baby Jesus a blanket?" I asked.

My grandson nodded happily, pointing now to the white felt tree skirt that wrapped around the base of the tree. I got a scissors, pulled a back corner of the skirt away from the tree and cut a small square. "Does this look good?"

He smiled, took the square of felt and laid it carefully on baby Jesus. Now, every year our Nativity scene has a square of white felt tucked around the baby Jesus. A notch is cut out of the back of the Christmas tree skirt. It is a reminder of the compassion my grandchildren are capable of showing.

FEELING ANOTHER'S PAIN

Perhaps I was so touched by my grandson's concern for the cold baby Jesus because I was seeing the dawning of empathy and compassion in him. Infants and small children are typically not much concerned with the feelings of others. They survive and thrive because they are self-centered. They do not care who they awaken in the middle of the night when they are hungry or uncomfortable. They are not worried about hurting someone's feelings by declaring they do not like something. They think only of what they want when they grab for a toy or a breakable knickknack.

Those who study early childhood development say it is around the age of eighteen months when a toddler can begin to understand feelings. I have seen that with my grandchildren. They have a set of shape and color matching eggs. Each egg has a different facial expression. By the time she was two years old, my granddaughter could tell me which egg was happy, sad, sleepy, or angry. She liked to point to pictures in the books we read and tell me, based on the facial expressions, whether the character was angry, scared, or worried.

When we see these tender shoots of empathy sprouting in our grandchildren, it is time for us to begin to teach them compassion. We can teach our grandchildren about empathy and compassion by talking with them about feelings. We can be sensitive to their feelings and encourage them to think about other people's feelings. We can model compassion for them by treating them and others with kindness and gentleness. We can ask them to consider what they might do to help a person who is feeling bad.

Empathy and compassion are not the same. Empathy is the ability to imagine how another person might feel in a particular situation. Compassion is feeling so strongly for what another person is going through that we feel called to action. Compassion does not mean we know or understand their feelings. We can have empathy without compassion or compassion without empathy. Or we can have them both. My grandson felt empathy for baby Jesus when he imagined he was cold. My grandson showed compassion when he wanted to make a blanket for him.

We may think our grandchildren are too young for compassion. We may want to protect them from the pain of the world. We may want to tell them not to worry about the cold infant Jesus, the homeless man on the street, or the victims of disasters flashed on television screens. Our grandchildren, however, are quite capable of understanding and caring.

Child psychologists also say that most four-year-old children are able to realize the impact their actions have on other people. They know their kindness will make someone happy; their selfishness will make someone sad; their screaming will scare a baby; their friendliness can make someone feel welcomed.

I have seen this to be true as well. One day, when we were all together for a family vacation on the lake, my son walked into the condo waving a wire-mesh container. "I've got crickets!" he announced. "Who wants to go fishing?"

My granddaughter was the first one to run to his side. He has taught her to be quite a little fisherman. She knew you almost always caught a fish with a cricket on your line. Within seconds everyone but me was heading out the door for some fishing. As they were piling into cars, my five-year-old granddaughter turned around and saw me waving by the door. "Grandma, aren't you coming?" she asked.

"No," I replied. "Grandma, doesn't like fishing."

"But you will be lonely," she cried and came running back to me. "I will stay here with you."

Here again was empathy combined with compassion. This little preschooler was quickly able to imagine what my emotions might be and to think that her leaving could be the cause of it. She compassionately wanted to do something to make me feel better and was willing to give up her own fun to make sure I was okay. Even though she was the first one who wanted to go fishing, she was willing to stay with me so I would not be sad. Only after we all convinced her Grandma had some work to do and would not be lonely did she regain her enthusiasm for the adventure.

So, if we had that understanding of feelings and emotions when we were mere toddlers, and if we could see how our actions might hurt someone else by the time we were four, what went wrong? Why isn't our world full of wonderful people who hate the thought of someone else being sad, lonely, hungry, or hurting? The answer quite simply is ego. As we get older, our capacity for empathy grows, but our motivation to "take care of number one" does too.

PUTTING ON COMPASSION

If during our life journey we paid close attention to the Gospels, perhaps we could set aside our ego and wrap ourselves in compassion. Saint Paul describes compassion as a cloak or a jacket we can wear. "Put on then, as God's chosen ones, holy and beloved, heartfelt compassion, kindness, humility, gentleness, and patience, bearing with one another and forgiving one another, if one has a grievance against another; as the Lord has forgiven you, so must you also do" (Col 3:12–13). This image of compassion as something we can put on is a lovely image. Wouldn't it be great if we could imagine ourselves simply picking up a beautiful coat and wrapping it around our shoulders whenever we were tempted to ignore or judge another person in need? Yet, as easily as we put on a cloak, we can throw it from our shoulders when it becomes uncomfortable. Now that we have grandchildren watching us, it might be a good time in our lives to wrap compassion around us more securely and fasten it with a strong clasp of prayer. We do not want it to slip from our shoulders as it might have once done. We want our grandchildren to always see us as people who care for those who suffer. In this way, we can help grow compassion in their young hearts.

If we doubt compassion is one of the most important virtues for us to nurture in our grandchildren, we need only look at Our Lord's teachings. In the Judgment of the Nations story, Jesus tells us very clearly how we will be judged (see Mt 25:31–45). We will not be judged on how much we prayed or how much we went to Mass. We will not be judged on how much we studied Scripture. We will certainly not be judged on how much money we made, how nice our home was, or how up-to-date our wardrobe was. We will simply be judged by how often we showed compassion. Jesus will call us to join him in eternal peace and joy if we fed the hungry, gave drink to the thirsty, or welcomed the stranger. He will open his arms to us if we provided clothing and shelter to the needy, cared for the sick, or visited those in prison. These acts of mercy are all the outpouring of compassion. For if we really feel compassion for another person we want to help them.

Compassion is not a passive emotion. It is a very active virtue. True compassion is empathy in action. If we are in pain or suffering, we act. Likewise, when we feel the pain and suffering of another, we want to take action.

CULTIVATING COMPASSION

We may naturally start to feel empathy as toddlers, but it takes great faith to practice the virtue of compassion in our self-centered society. It is so much easier to keep the focus on ourselves, look the other way, or deny another person is in need. We learn to convince ourselves this child is not cold or that old person is not lonely. Eventually we become numb to the suffering around us. Our Information Age is partly to blame for this numbness. Today, the hurts and pains of the world are flashed before our eyes so often on news shows, the Internet, and social media that we just stop seeing them. The needs seem overwhelming. What can one person do? Ronald Reagan once said, "No one can help everyone, but everyone can help someone." Compassion is an extremely personal act. We don't have to fix the world. We just have to care for the people God places in our path.

We need two things to practice compassion. The first is God's grace. Let us ask God every day to open our eyes to one person who needs our help and then give us the grace to do what is necessary. The second thing we need is acceptance. We need to see that all people are just like us. They feel the same pain we feel. They have the same range of emotions. The mother holding a starving infant on the dusty streets of a Third World country feels just as much worry and pain as the mother holding a sick child in the sterile emergency room of a modern hospital. Once we begin to realize we are emotionally wired the same, then we start to know real compassion. When we open ourselves to the possibility of truly suffering with the person who is hungry, grieving, lonely, sick, or scared, we become ready to take action.

LOOKING INTO THE FACE OF JESUS

We learn compassion not only by seeing ourselves in a suffering person, but also by seeing Jesus there. It is sweet and sentimental to look at the angelic baby Jesus in a crib and put a blanket on him. It is not as charming to look into the bloodied face of Jesus on the cross. Yet, this is where we must look if we want to become more compassionate. We must gaze at the suffering Christ on the cross. Imagine the blood dripping from his wounds. Feel the pain of his every breath. And then remember *why* he suffered like this. He did it for love, and to give us the grace to be better and more compassionate people. He did it to save us from our sins of indifference.

We cannot truly adore the infant in the crib if we are not also willing to follow the man on the cross. Saint Thérèse of Lisieux, known as the Little Flower, is a witness to this. We call her Saint Thérèse of the Child Jesus and think of her as a gentle and humble little saint. But the full religious name the Carmelite order bestowed on her was Sister Thérèse of the Child Jesus and the Holy Face. The Holy Face is the suffering face of Christ Veronica wiped with a towel. It is the face that was crowned with thorns. It is the face that cried out, "Father, forgive them, they know not what they do" (Lk 23:34).

We, too, are often guilty of not knowing what we are doing. Often, we are not aware of how our actions or words cause pain to others. But for the sake of our grandchildren, we need to start paying greater attention. We need to learn to see the suffering Jesus in the face of every suffering person. If the world is going to be a better place, it will only be because more people are showing compassion for one another.

We can also cultivate more compassion in our grandchildren by encouraging them to think about how another person might feel and to consider whether there is anything they could do to make that person feel better. Depending on our different circumstances, we all have opportunities to expose our grandchildren to those who need compassion. When my mother was in a nursing home, my brother and sister-in-law regularly took their granddaughter to visit her. The little girl quickly became comfortable being in the presence of the sick. She could look into the face of the people she saw and not back away. No doubt she will always be compassionate to the elderly and sick.

My mother-in-law is 102. My grandchildren regularly see Great-Grandma here at our home and like to share their toys with her. Recently, my husband and I sponsored a five-year-old girl in a developing country. Her picture is on our refrigerator. I tell my granddaughter about this little girl who wants to learn to read but has no books. We color pictures for her and send her some of our stickers.

Even if face-to-face work with the needy is not possible for us or our grandchildren, we can still include people who are homeless, immigrants, those who are sick or dying, and the many who are lonely in our daily prayers. Through her great devotion to the Holy Face of Jesus and her prayers for missionaries, Saint Thérèse of Lisieux became a saint without ever going beyond the walls of her convent.

Our pastor recommends we pray every day for the three Ds. There are those who are *distant* from us. They may be living in countries and conditions far away from the blessings we know. There are those who are *different* from us. They may have different backgrounds, opportunities, or health conditions. And there are those who are **difficult** for us. They may annoy us or cause us to judge harshly. If we pray for these people, we will grow in compassion for them.

The ways to help our grandchildren feel and act on compassion are endless. "A virtue is an habitual and firm disposition to do the good. It allows the person not only to perform good acts, but to give the best of himself" (*Catechism of the Catholic Church*, 1803). If we can make a habit out of showing compassion when we are with our grandchildren, we will be instilling that virtue in them for a lifetime.

For Reflection

1. Do I notice, praise, and encourage the times when my grandchildren show empathy or act with compassion?

2. Understanding the feelings of others is the basis of all compassion. Do I talk with my grandchildren about the feelings of others — those people we encounter in books, movies, or real-life situations?

3. Do I expose my grandchildren to situations that call for compassion, or do I try to protect them from the pain and misery of the world?

4. "What would Jesus do?" was a popular slogan for youth groups several years ago. Do I ever talk with my grandchildren about the way Jesus cared for people who were hungry, sick, poor, or outcast? Do I remind them this is what Jesus wants us to do, too?

A Grandparent's Prayer

Dear Jesus, you continually call us to compassion. Help us to be more aware of those who need our compassion every day. Inspire us to model compassion for our grandchildren so they will grow up knowing how to serve you by feeding those who are hungry, giving drink to those who are thirsty, and caring for those who suffer. Help us to set a compassionate example for our dear grandchildren. Thank you for hearing this prayer. Amen.

Chapter 4

Service

I passed a neighbor the other day on my morning walk. She is an amazing grandparent. She and her husband babysit every day so her daughter and son-in-law can work without placing their child in day care. As I was admiring her darling grandson she told me she was dreading the day. She had to take the little guy to the doctor because he needed his shots.

SERVICE TO OUR FAMILIES

The amount of service this generation of grandparents gives in caring for their grandchildren is incredible. Everywhere we go we see grandparents tending their children's children. They are at the grocery store, the playground, the library, restaurants, and morning Mass. Grandparents today buy car seats, strollers, high chairs, and toys — all so their grandchildren will be safe and happy when they are with their grandparents. The Pew Research Center says that, in 2015, 94 percent of grandparents helped provide some care for their grandchildren — 22 percent provided regular care; 72 percent provided occasional care.

Gone are the days when grandparents say: "I raised my children. I am *not* doing it again." And today's families often need our support. In more than 50 percent of two-parent homes, both the mother and father work full-time jobs, according to Pew. Although mothers have traditionally been the primary caregiver for children, today 70 percent of mothers are in the workforce full or part time. In 40 percent of households mothers are the primary breadwinner in the family. Young parents — both mothers and fathers — often work long days and demanding schedules. They are sharing more equally in all home and child-care responsibilities. Many of these young families turn to grandparents for support and help.

We often think of service as something we do outside of the home or family. Certainly, volunteering in our parishes, food pantries, hospitals, homeless shelters, and even overseas missions is an important part of living our Christian faith. Yet, as my mother would often tell me, charity begins at home. Today grandparents are being called back, in large numbers, to serve in their own homes. Many grandfathers as well as grandmothers are now "stay-at-home" grandparents. In my neighborhood, retired teachers, executives, fire captains, and supervisors can all be seen pushing a stroller or following a toddler just learning to peddle a tricycle. Many retired grandparents dedicate a couple of days a week to the grandchildren and a couple of days a week to volunteering in some other charitable work. In addition, modern grandparents are often called upon to care for elderly relatives. Pope Francis, when in Philadelphia in 2015, reminded us of the importance of this work by pointing out, "A people incapable of caring for children and caring for the elderly is a people without a future."

This service to the youngest and the oldest in our families is a way to carry out the corporal works of mercy. We feed our family members. We may help them get dressed. We stay with them when they are sick. And although transportation was not one of the original works of mercy Jesus mentioned in the Gospels, it could be added to the list in today's world. One grandmother I know drives forty-five minutes each way to pick up a grandson from soccer practice twice a week because the practice schedule conflicts with his parents' work schedule. Without his grandmother's service, this boy would not be able to participate in the sport.

Parents and grandchildren are not the only ones who benefit from the service we may offer our families. We grandparents may benefit, too. "The only ones among you who will be really happy are those who have sought and found how to serve," the famous philosopher and physician Albert Schweitzer once said. When we serve in our families, we really do become happier. We have the opportunity to establish a special bond with our grandchildren that can last a lifetime.

In his departing remarks during his visit to the United States in 2015, Pope Francis said, "Your care for one another is care for Jesus himself." What a blessing it is for us to care for Jesus by caring for our grandchildren. When we understand the grace of service, we realize how important it is to teach our grandchildren this virtue through every stage of their lives.

TEACHING SERVICE TO CHILDREN

Children do not always like the idea of service. Play is much more fun for them. I understand. I love playing with my grandchildren. I like toys with lots of pieces. My grandchildren's room at my house is full of blocks, puzzles, building sets, and beads. So, when my grandchildren come over, we inevitably make a mess all over the house. I was not initially very good at making them clean up. We simply would go from one activity to another, leaving a trail of towers, completed puzzles, and imaginary play scenes in our wake. Often, they wanted to save their creations to show their parents. I figured I would rather spend my time playing with them than picking up and would clean up myself after they left. But then my daughter-in-law asked me to support them in teaching their children that they have a responsibility to clean up after themselves. Now I try harder to encourage my grandchildren to clean the messes they make.

Children need to learn they have a responsibility to serve in their family. It is the stepping stone to service in their community. If children do not learn to do for themselves what they are capable of doing, they soon start to believe everything should be done for them. They grow to expect everyone to wait on them and do everything for them. When children are encouraged to help pick up toys, prepare a meal, or keep a younger sibling happy, they learn they can do good and useful things in life. They learn that they have something to contribute to the well-being of others.

Of course, it helps if we can make chores fun for them. Our yard contains many old trees, so, after a storm, the grass is littered with sticks that have blown from the trees. For safety's sake, we must gather up these sticks before we play outside. My grandchildren have found it fun to pick up the sticks and pretend they are building a bonfire. They have also challenged each other to see who could find the biggest stick or who could throw a stick the farthest into the woods. Turning service into a game helps them learn that service can be rewarding in many ways.

By encouraging our grandchildren to give small acts of service, we can help them see that being helpful can make them feel good. Asking them to carry a dish to the sink, throw some paper in the trash, or retrieve an item from another room are all ways to introduce them to service. When we praise them for these simple tasks, they begin to feel the warm glow that comes from helping. Providing service also helps build self-esteem. When a person — even a child — is able to offer a helping hand, they realize they have value and are able to make an important contribution. We can also teach our grandchildren that service is a pathway to sainthood.

Saint Bernadette was fourteen years old when she was sent out to gather firewood for her family. It was while she was providing this service that the Blessed Mother appeared to her for the first time. The three children at Fátima were also giving service to their families by tending their sheep when the Blessed Mother came to them. They were even younger than Bernadette. Lucia was ten. Francisco was nine. Jacinta was seven. In the many messages the Blessed Mother gave to these saintly children, she never once said they were too young to serve.

The best model for service, however, is Our Lord's good friend Martha. Through service, Martha of Bethany made her home so warm and welcoming that Jesus stopped there often to visit. Today, Saint Martha is the patron saint for all those who serve. While our grandchildren may not yet have the zeal for service Martha had, it is important to remind them how good it is to serve their family and the greater community. Often, as they get older, they will want to show they are growing up by how well they can undertake a variety of chores.

When my grandson was three years old, he had the idea one day that we should build a town across the family room floor with all the blocks and all his little metal cars. (I told you we make big messes when we play!) He scurried up the stairs to retrieve his basket of cars and the bags of plastic building blocks. As we were gathering everything up to take downstairs he was struggling with two large bags of blocks while I had been assigned to carry the small basket of cars and another bag of blocks. When he got to the stairs, I told him we should switch; I would carry the big bags, and he could carry the little basket. As he began his slow and careful descent down the stairs, one hand holding the banister and the other clutching the basket, he informed me: "It's okay, Grandma, if I carry the little stuff because I am little and you are big. But when I get big and you get old then I will carry the big stuff and you can carry the little stuff. Right, Grandma?" I assured him that would not only be right but also wonderful.

Let us teach our grandchildren to take pride in service so they will be willing to help both their families and the world, however they may be needed.

FINDING TIME

One of the biggest challenges to being people of service in this busy world is time. We say, "I don't **have** time." Yet all of us have the exact same 1,440 minutes each day. Some people waste those minutes in self-serving or lazy ways. Other people accomplish amazing things in those same number of minutes. For most of us, the 1,440 minutes tick away in a mixture of productive and unproductive moments. This is not a bad thing, as long as we are using some of those minutes to serve God, help others, and make the world a better place for our grandchildren.

The mistake we make is thinking we don't have enough time to give some of it to serving others. That is simply not true. God gives each of us the exact amount of time we need to do the work he has planned for us. We just need to get our priorities in order.

All time belongs to God. Our minutes are on loan to us from the Great Creator of All Time. It is as foolish for us to think we own time as for us to think we own any of God's great creations. We do not own the sea, the stars, the sun, or the rain. Likewise, we do not own time. When we think of time as our own, we think we can do whatever we want with it. We begin to resent anything or anyone who infringes on *our* time. God, however, continually calls us to use the time he is loaning us in service.

We might want to respond by saying, "I can't *find* time." Of course we can't. There is no place on earth where we can find more time. There is no "time" store in the mall. We can't order more time online. We won't find time hidden in some far-off place. We can't borrow time from our neighbors or steal it from a stranger on the street. We won't find time lying lost on a parking lot, where someone else accidentally dropped it. The only time we have is right this minute.

Ideally, we are able to use a portion of our time each day in service to our families, including our grandchildren, and to the world they will inherit. To do this, it is helpful to turn to God, the creator of our time, and ask him how he wants us to use the time he has entrusted to us. This is one of the primary purposes for morning and evening prayer. It helps us to use the time God has given us in service to God's wishes.

SERVING IN THE VINEYARD

When we ask God what we should do with the minutes and hours of our days, we will invariably hear the reply, "You too go into my vineyard" (Mt 20:4). Our Lord repeats this command twice in the parable about the workers in the vineyard (see Mt 20:1–16). It is the story of a master who goes to the marketplace repeatedly through the day, inviting people to come work in his vineyard. It is the story of our own lives. In every stage of our lives, God calls us to service. It is never too late for us to go into God's vineyard. We can take fresh inspiration from this story if we ever find ourselves wasting too much time. At one point in the story the master asks, "Why do you stand here idle?" (v. 6). Let us hope God does not have to ask us, on Judgement Day, why we stood idle so often throughout our lives.

I once saw a poster of Jesus washing the feet of his disciples on the night of the Last Supper. After providing the most lowly and humble service of washing the feet of his friends, Jesus told them they must go out into the world and do likewise. At the bottom of the poster, in bold letters, were the words, "If money could save the world, God could have just sent a check."

God did not send a check. He sent his Son, who fed the hungry, cared for the sick, and cried with Martha and Mary as they grieved the death of their brother Lazarus. Throughout his ministry on earth, up until the very night before his death, Jesus called us to do the same. Service is one of the strongest themes that runs through all four Gospels:

"Amen, I say to you, what you did not do for one of these least ones, you did not do for me." (Matthew 25:45)

"If anyone wishes to be first, he shall be the last of all and the servant of all." (Mark 9:35)

"If anyone wishes to come after me, he must deny himself and take up his cross daily and follow me." (Luke 9:23)

"Amen, amen, I say to you, whoever believes in me will do the works that I do." (John 14:12)

Giving ourselves in service is a way of taking up our cross and following Jesus. Saint Francis of Assisi had a strong love of the cross. He meditated on it daily. He taught that the vertical beam represents God reaching down to us and us reaching up to God; and the horizontal beam represents God reaching out to others through us. If our life is only about reaching up to God or only about reaching out to others, we do not have a cross. We just have one plank of wood. It is when we combine our love for God with service to others that we are truly living the Gospel as Jesus taught it to us.

We can teach this message to our grandchildren through the service we give them and in what we share with them about what we do for others. It may not be appropriate to take our grandchildren with us when we serve in our church and community, yet we can make them aware of what we are doing and why. When they are young, they look up to us. Let them look up to a person who is giving service.

When I am getting ready to leave my grandchildren's house, they often beg me not to go. One day my grandson was begging me to stay, sprinkling his pleas with his favorite word, "Why?"

"Why you have to go, Grandma? Why?"

"Because Grandma has a meeting?"

"Why you have a meeting?"

I was working on a committee to help turn a closed school into a senior living center. Giving him a simplified version of this work, I replied. "Grandma is helping to build new homes for old people."

"Why, Grandma? Why they need new homes?"

"Because sometimes they fall and get hurt in their old houses," I answered.

"Oh," my grandson replied, sadly giving me a good-bye kiss and hug. No more questions. I was free to go. In that moment, I think he understood the value of service.

Service can be hard work. Caring for our grand-children may conflict with our plans, zap our energy, strain our backs, and leave us exhausted. Serving in the community may at times be frustrating, taxing, and un-appreciated. Whatever kind of service we do, it usually involves some sacrifice. That is good. The word sacrifice comes from the Latin words that mean "to make holy." We can make our lives holier by serving our families and others. In one of his prayers Saint Ignatius of Loyola en-courages us "to give and not to count the cost." That does not mean we should overextend ourselves or neglect our own family responsibilities to give service to others. But if the cost of service is to give up some television time, In-ternet surfing, or idleness, it is certainly a cost not worth counting. When we generously serve, we may discover nothing matters now as much as journeying with our grandchildren and others in need.

For Reflection

1. Am I sensitive enough to the tremendous burdens young families carry today? Do I try to assist where possible with the many demands on their schedules? Or do I add to their burdens with my own demands?

2. Do I do too much for my grandchildren, denying them the good feelings that come from serving rather than being served?

3. How do I see time? Do I think it is something I deserve to selfishly enjoy? Or do I realize it is a gift God has entrusted to me so I can serve his people?

4. Do I plan and balance well the service I give to family, Church, and community? Is there an area where God might be calling me to be more generous with my time?

A Grandparent's Prayer

Dearest Jesus, through my witness, help me to inspire my grandchildren to be people of service. Guide me in encouraging them to be helpful and caring. Let them never hear me complain about the service you call me to do. Let them see me as a person who is always happy to help. May they learn from me to follow your call for us to be servants to one another. Thank you for hearing this prayer. Amen.

Chapter 5

Sharing

A friend once invited me over while she was babysitting her two-year-old grandson. He was a sweet little boy who loved playing with little toy cars. He had a basket full of them. As I tried to make friends with this little guy, my friend and I coaxed him to let me see one of his cars. At first, he clutched it tightly to his chest and hid behind his grandmother. As he became braver, he edged closer to me and handed me the car. I oohed and aahed over it. He thought that was great. Laughing and giggling, he began to bring me one new car after another. Each time I showed a level of excitement that pleased him, he clapped and danced with glee. Before I knew it, I had every one of his dozens of miniature toy cars in my lap.

When he realized he was out of cars, however, he was not happy. He stomped over to me, began to grab the cars away and throw them back toward his basket. He wanted everything back which he had just given to me. He was tired of sharing.

THE AMBIGUITY OF SHARING

We all have ambiguous feelings about sharing. Sharing can be the basis of many wonderful experiences. We love to share special holidays and occasions with family. We like to sit around a warm fire and share a bottle of wine with friends. We enjoy sharing our tips for the best restaurant, movie, or book. Yet, sharing is not so fun when the book or tool is never returned, when the time is inconvenient, or when we have other plans.

In the parable of the talents (see Mt 25:14–30), Jesus calls us to share in two ways. First, the servants are challenged to share their time and skills to earn the master a good return on his investment. Those who are successful at this level of sharing are richly rewarded. They are invited to, "Come, share your master's joy" (v. 21). These are perhaps some of the most beautiful and promising words in Scripture. How we all long to hear Our Lord invite us to share his joy when we meet him face to face. Good sharing will help us earn that reward. But how good are we at sharing?

Like the child with his little cars, we were all taught to share when we were young. And today we may consider it a virtue we have mastered. Yet, we might be like the farmer in an old fable. This farmer liked to imagine how generous he would be if he were rich. He was so obsessed with this thought that one night he dreamed an angel asked him what he would do if God showered thousands of dollars upon him. The man immediately replied he would give half to God. The angel then asked the man what he would do if he was given a large mansion. The man replied he would invite the poor to live there with him. Then the angel asked if his neighbor could borrow his horse. The farmer immediately said no. The angel asked the man why he was so eager to share money and a large house but not his old horse. The man replied: "I can only imagine what it is like to have more money than I need and a large mansion. But, I know what it is like to have only one horse. I need him. I cannot share him with anyone." I have to admit I was a little like that old man with my first grandchild.

SHARING FAMILY

Marriage does not just join two people; it joins two families. When a grandchild is born, at least two sets of grandparents — if not more — are joined together. Then there are two sides of aunts and uncles, great-grandparents, and special friends. It adds up to be many people who have one thing in common. They all want a share of the little one we call our grandchild.

A single friend of mine never had children. She built a good life around her career and stayed close to her married siblings. She never really missed not having children. But now, as her nieces and nephews are getting married and starting families, she says she feels a desire to be a grandmother. Fortunately, her family is close and they love to share the little ones with her and use her for babysitting. She calls this new generation of nieces and nephews her "grands."

We might be happy to welcome a new son or daughter, and thrilled to welcome a new grandchild, but sharing our children and grandchildren with another family can be a challenge. Pope Francis addresses the challenge of blending families in his apostolic exhortation on love in the family: "One particularly delicate aspect of love is learning not to view these relatives as somehow competitors, threats, or intruders" (*The Joy of Love*, 198). Having a grandchild is a family experience; it is not a private experience between just grandparent and grandchild. Hopefully, all family members want to share together the joy of this new generation.

I was not, at first, very good at this sharing. I wanted my grandchildren to know and love their aunt and uncles, but I also wanted exclusive rights when they were in my home. I was grateful my grandchildren had such wonderful grandparents on their mother's side of the family, but when we are all together for baptisms and birthdays, we had to balance which grandparent held, cared for, or fed the little one. And I had trouble respecting the parents' rights to care for their child when they were in my home. This was especially difficult because when I babysat I was the main caregiver. So, even when we were all together, my maternal instinct still kicked in when a grandchild cried or asked for something. I needed to learn to let Mommy and Daddy be the "first responders" when we were together.

Realizing my grandchildren needed all these wonderful people in their lives helped me step back and enjoy watching other family members interacting with my grandchildren. I knew each of us brought different gifts and strengths to my grandchild. My daughter loves summer and pools; I do not like the sun or swimming. So, she takes her nieces and nephew swimming. My grandchildren's other grandmother has a great love for horses; I am not a big animal lover. She teaches them the wonder of God's four-legged creatures with a gentleness that comes from a woman who works with horses. They love getting to visit her and to ride her horse.

My unmarried daughter is also amazingly generous with sharing the childhood toys she has saved. I thought she might want to keep them packed away in case she later has a little girl of her own. She, however, was quick to share all her childhood things with her little goddaughter. One of the best days we had together was getting her old, little toy horses out of the attic, then washing and brushing out their hair so they would be nice and clean for the next generation to enjoy. The day my daughter brought the cleaned horses out for my granddaughter, she and my daughter-in-law and granddaughter were like three little girls playing together on the floor. It was fun to watch.

A great example of family sharing came from four grandparents who shared the care of their new first-born granddaughter. Although the mother was able to negotiate five months of maternity leave, because of the baby's frail condition the pediatrician was not comfortable placing the baby in day care until the little one was six months old. All four grandparents came to the rescue. Each one took one week to care for the baby. This made the transition back to work easier for the new mom and for the grandchild. The story is more inspiring because the young family lived out of town. Thus each grandparent took vacation time to travel to the family's home and live there for a week.

I felt the blessings of being in a sharing family when my mother died. My daughter-in-law was eight-and-a-half months pregnant with their third child at the time. Yet, she called me and asked if I would like to see my grandchildren. She thought they might ease my sadness. We spent a lovely afternoon together. Because she knew it would mean much to me, she made sure my four-and two-year-old grandchildren were there at the wake and the funeral. This was no small gift of sharing from a woman whose advanced pregnancy could have easily been a reason to stay home with the toddlers! I will always treasure her kindness.

She is very good about sharing family because she grew up in a family that shared well. She often tells me she wants her children to have a close and special relationship with me, because she enjoyed and treasured such a relationship with her grandmother. Her kindness toward me is evidence of the fact that how we share and interact with our extended family will have a profound impact on future generations — on our grandchildren's interaction with their own children and grandchildren. I will be forever grateful to the women in her family who taught my daughter-in-law to share her children with others so graciously. I hope someday a woman I do not yet know will be grateful for the example I have tried to set in my own family.

TRADITION, TRADITION!

Letting go of our family traditions can be another difficult sharing challenge for some grandparents. Many of us have grown up with the idealized Norman Rockwell images of three generations gathered around Christmas trees and Thanksgiving tables. Those images might include grandparents standing on the front porch to welcome their children and grandchildren into their home. Yet, these imagined scenes rarely include the "other" grandparents. It ignores the fact that young families have a lot to juggle when it comes to holiday celebrations and family traditions.

We need to step back and let them make the plans that work best for them. Pope Francis stresses this when writing about families: "We encounter problems whenever we think that relationships or people ought to be perfect, or when we put ourselves at the center and expect things to turn out our way.... We will end up incapable of living together, antisocial, unable to control our impulses, and our families will become battlegrounds ... other people also have a right to live in this world, just as they are. It does not matter if they hold me back, if they unsettle my plans, or annoy me by the way they act or think, or if they are not everything I want them to be" (*The Joy of Love*, 92).

Young families will often upset the plans and traditions we may have treasured for many years. We may discover it is time to share new traditions. For years, our neighborhood had a Halloween potluck dinner. As our children outgrew family Halloweens, the adults still gathered together. Gradually, some began to bring their grandchildren. When my own grandchildren started trick-or-treating, though, their parents understandably wanted them to trick-or-treat in their own neighborhood with their own friends. We started a new Halloween tradition. Now we gather for Halloween at their home. My son builds a fire in his firepit. Grandpa and I and my single son and daughter sit around the fire and give out candy to the neighborhood kids while Mom and Dad get to trick-or-treat together with their children. It is different from what we had, but it is becoming a tradition, too.

Some changes, however, may be more difficult to accept. Most of us don't envision Grandma and Grandpa sitting alone for a holiday. It is, however, a reality we might have to accept, especially if family members are scattered around the country or work 24/7 jobs. We must resist the temptation to behave in selfish, spoiled, sulking, or demanding ways. It is important to share and play nice in our extended families. Remember: Our grandchildren will be watching us.

SHARING WHO WE ARE

Another sharing dilemma some grandparents may agonize over is what they will be called by their grandchildren. They want a name that is unique to them. Some do not want to share their grandparent title with anyone else. This can become an unnecessary source of stress between parents and grandparents, especially if one or the other wants a name the other strongly dislikes. In the end, most grandparents are known simply as Grandma, Grandpa, Nana, or Papa. If we don't like the term grandma or grandpa, we should consider the alternatives. It seems this term became popular in thirteenth-century Europe. Prior to that, grandparents were referred to as "olderfather" or "oldermother." I think I like "grand" better than "older." So, let us not fight over what we are called and recognize that a little creativity may be in order.

If a special name develops, it is often the grandchildren who create it. My favorite is the name my cousin Nancy's grandchildren call her. Grandma Nancy became "Grancy." For a while I was afraid I might become "Grandma Dum Dum" because of my habit of giving my grandchildren a small Dum Dum lollipop for a treat. It got to the point every time my grandson saw me he would say, "Grandma, Dum Dum?" For him it was a question, asking in his baby talk if he could have a treat. But his older sister thought it was a hilarious name for me. Fortunately, that did not stick.

At the end of the day, worrying about what our grandchildren will call us and how we will be differentiated from other grandparents and great-grandparents in the family is not important. Whatever name our grandchildren call us should be music to our ears. The simple fact that they know us is all that matters.

A WORLD IN NEED OF SHARING

It is extremely important for our grandchildren to know that we are people who are willing to share in many ways. Our world today very much needs sharing. A key document of the Second Vatican Council states, "Many persons are quite aggressively demanding those benefits of which with vivid awareness they judge themselves to be deprived either through injustice or unequal distribution" (*Gaudium et Spes*, Pastoral Constitution on the Church in the Modern World, 9). Fifty years later, due to advancements in communication and technology, underprivileged people are even more acutely aware of the disparity in our world.

From a spiritual perspective, the secret to sharing freely is in recognizing all we have is a gift from God. God has entrusted great gifts to us so we can know the joy of sharing and of learning how to care for one another. I try to teach this concept to my grandchildren through the way we handle toys at our house.

Because I like playing with my grandchildren, we have lots of toys. When I had just one grandchild, she naturally believed the toys were hers. When her brother came along, she began to claim some of the favorite toys as hers. I quickly informed her all the toys were mine. They may enjoy them when they are visiting, but they do not own them. They cannot take them home, nor can they take them from one another.

Our world is like a grandparents' house. Nothing belongs only to us. Like a grandparent, God is happy to see us enjoy the blessings he has given us, but he also wants us to share our blessings with others. For the sake of their future, we must model and teach this message to our grandchildren.

For Reflection

1. Am I gracious in sharing my grandchildren with their other grandparents, aunts, and uncles? Do I recognize the blessings they can share with my grandchildren?

2. Have I consciously or unconsciously tried to impose my own ways on my family rather than sharing the planning of family celebrations and holidays?

3. Are there ways I can help my grandchildren see that sharing can be fun rather than a burden to be endured?

4. How well do I accept the basic truth expressed in the Psalms, "The earth is the LORD's and all it holds, / the world and those who dwell in it" (Ps 24:1)? How can knowing that everything belongs to God help me do a better job of sharing my blessings?

A Grandparent's Prayer

Thank you, dear God, for the many good people who surround, support, and care for my grandchildren. Help all the members of our merged and extended families work together for the benefit of my grandchildren. May we model Christian sharing in all our activities. May our sharing of the blessings you have entrusted to us help pave the way for a future world which is kinder, more just, and more compassionate to all people. Please hear this prayer. Amen.

Chapter 6

Awe

My youngest granddaughter learned to reach for the doorknobs on the exterior doors of our house when she was just sixteen months old. She had no interest in closet doors or interior room doors, but she was forever wanting to go outside. She was just like her older sister and brother. Ever since they were babies, my grandchildren have loved the outdoors. My oldest granddaughter used to climb up on the sofa to look outside all the time. When I carried her outside, she would reach for the leaves on low-hanging tree branches. Her brother loved being outside at night. Taking "night walks" was one of our favorite things to do when he and his sister joined us for an evening. "Moon" is one of the first words I can remember him saying clearly.

I do not know where this great love of nature comes from in them. Maybe they have inherited their parents' love of the outdoors. Maybe, though, it is a natural inclination for all children to want to be close to the things God created. Certainly, awe and wonder should be traits we would want to nurture in our grandchildren. They can bring them closer to God.

THE WONDER OF NATURE

Pope Francis tells us in his encyclical on the environment, *Laudato Si'*, "We were not meant to be inundated by cement, asphalt, glass, and metal and deprived of physical contact with nature" (*On Care for Our Common Home*, 44). In the Book of Genesis, we see the great care and attention God gave to carefully crafting, day by day, a world that would be absolutely perfect for us. Modern science tells us that a "creation day" for God might have been tens of thousands or millions of years. This truth makes the wonder of nature and the love God put into creating this world for us even more awesome. Yet, today, we so often choose to spend our time in places and things that inspire little or no awe in us.

Awe is a mixture of reverence, fear, and wonder caused by something majestic, sublime, or sacred. We don't often feel awe while shopping in a mall, playing video games, texting and tweeting, watching a sporting event, or going to an amusement park. In our culture, it seems we prefer to admire from a distance. We sit at our computers in our man-made structures and admire videos of beautiful landscapes and animals in the wild. Yet, we rarely venture out. Perhaps at some level we have become afraid of awe and wonder.

Children, however, have no fear of awe. They live with it constantly. To them, the many things we take for granted are new and wonderful. As grandparents, we hopefully have the chance and the time to once again see the world through the amazed eyes of a child.

Down the street from our house is a large willow tree. I drive by it many times a day, hardly noticing it. Once when I had my two-year-old granddaughter in the car, she yelled for me to stop as we passed that tree. I thought something was wrong. Instead, she said in total awe: "Grandma, look at that tree! It has really long hair!" She wanted to get out of the car immediately and run through its hair. Still, to this day, my grandchildren call the willow tree "the hair tree." Visits to my house often include a walk down to this awesome tree, where my grandchildren giggle and run through the soft, low-hanging branches.

Another experience of innocent awe occurred while walking along a trail with my three-year-old grandson. He suddenly yanked on my hand, stopped, and said, "Grandma, let's look at this bug!"

He crouched down as close as he could get to the ground while still holding my hand. I crouched down next to him expecting to see some amazing insect. Instead, it was just a very normal, little bug walking along a stone.

"Do you see his wings?" my grandson asked.

"Yes," I answered. "They are very tiny." If I had been walking along by myself, I would have never noticed the bug, much less its little wings.

"What color are those wings, Grandma?" he asked. Good question. They were iridescent, shifting colors in the sunlight.

"I don't know," I answered, "maybe green, or yellow."

"I think they are blue," my grandson wisely answered. How amazing, I wonder, is a God who takes time to paint the wings of a tiny bug with such fine strokes of color?

After a few more minutes of simply watching the bug walk along the craggy rock my grandson had another question.

"Where you think he's going?" he asked.

"I don't know," I answered, "maybe home."

"Back to his mommy," my grandson agreed. That is where we all long to go. Back to the people who love us most.

Taking time to explore the wonder and beauty of nature is a wonderful way to introduce our grandchildren to the awesomeness of God. The eighteenth-century French philosopher Voltaire, although critical of the Catholic Church at the time, was a great believer in God. He once said, "I cannot imagine how the clockwork of the universe can exist without a clockmaker."

The Church also sees nature as a sure sign of a God who loves and cares for us. "The order, harmony, and beauty of the world point to an intelligent Creator" (*U.S. Catholic Catechism for Adults*, 32).

Half-inch iridescent wings just don't happen accidentally. Our grandchildren seem to naturally know that. How else do you explain such simple wonder and beauty? Pope Francis offers an answer: "Creation can only be understood as a gift from the outstretched hand of the Father" (*On Care for Our Common Home*, 76). What a beautiful image Francis paints of God reaching out his mighty hand to offer us a golden sunset, a pink- and violet-painted dawn, a pair of fluttering butterflies, or a perfect snowflake landing on our windshield. How often do we take all these simple gifts from God for granted? How often are we watching a television, computer, or phone screen instead of watching God's sky? Our grandchildren call us to notice and appreciate all the wonders of God's creation.

"Look, Grandma," my granddaughter exclaimed during a morning walk, "the moon is still out and it is the middle of the day. Silly moon!" She looked up at the sky and shouted: "Go to bed, moon! You are going to be tired tonight."

Let us walk often with our grandchildren through nature, so we can become reacquainted with the glory of God's creation ourselves. As we marvel at the care God has taken in every little detail, let us remember Our Lord's words: "Learn from the way the wild flowers grow. They do not work or spin. But I tell you that not even Solomon in all his splendor was clothed like one of them. If God so clothes the grass of the field, which grows today and is thrown into the oven tomorrow, will he not much more provide for you, O you of little faith?" (Mt 6:28–30).

THEOLOGY IN GEOLOGY

The many elements of nature can teach us much about our God. Rocks are one of my favorite natural treasures. Each one is unique. Many of them have little sparkles in them which we don't notice until we pick them up and look at them more closely. In that way, they are a lot like people.

My dad introduced me to rock collecting when I was a little girl. To this day, my ideal souvenir from any vacation is a rock. They are the cheapest mementos you can find and truly a piece of any place you have been. In the Old Testament, after he was cured by Elisha from his leprosy, Naaman asked Elisha if he could take "two mule-loads" of dirt home with him so he could pray on the same ground where Elisha worshiped God (see 2 Kgs 5:1–17). For me, taking a small rock from a beautiful place is the same idea, but much easier to get on a plane. I have rocks I've picked up from one of the highest peaks in the Rocky Mountains, the shores of the Great Lakes, the Oregon coast, and the Gulf of Mexico. Sometimes, when I am praying, I will hold one of my rocks and imagine being back in one of God's most awesome places.

One of my favorite rocks is a ruffled, heart-shaped piece of gravel my son found for me many years ago when we were hiking in a dry riverbed. Today, my granddaughter, who now knows hearts are a sign of love, likes to find heart-shaped rocks for me. I have a special collection of such rocks she has found. Each one reminds me of the promise God made to us through the prophet Ezekiel: "I will give you a new heart, and a new spirit I will put within you. I will remove the heart of stone from your flesh and give you a heart of flesh" (Ez 36:26).

Both nature and grandchildren have the power to soften our hearts. Put them together and you have an unbeatable combination — good for the heart and the soul. We come to know God in so many ways when we spend time in the natural world. This holy space offers us silence and power, majesty and miracles, tiny details and breathtaking expanses. Time spent admiring a bubbling brook, a majestic mountain, or the wings of a butterfly can be so much better for us than time spent in front of a television set, shopping in a mall, or at an amusement park.

The Psalms encourage us to share the awe of God's creation with our grandchildren: "Great is the LORD and worthy of much praise, / whose grandeur is beyond understanding. / One generation praises your deeds to the next / and proclaims your mighty works. / They speak of the splendor of your majestic glory, / tell of your wonderful deeds. / They speak of the power of your awesome acts / and recount your great deeds" (Ps 145:3–6). Let us be a generation which proclaims to our grandchildren the awe and wonder of God's creation.

THE CARE OF NATURE

Once we see the beauty and power of nature through the eyes of our grandchildren, we can understand and more fully embrace Pope Francis's plea to be good stewards of our environment. He has been insistent in telling us that care for the environment is an essential part of living out our Christian faith. In his address at the White House during his 2015 visit to the United States, Pope Francis pleaded: "When it comes to the care of our 'common home' we are living at a critical moment in history. We still have time to make the changes needed."

In addition, speaking at the 2015 Festival of Families in Philadelphia, Pope Francis urged us to consider the environment: "God made this wonderful world in which we live and which, since we are not too smart, we are now in the process of destroying."

This is an issue all families, all parents, and all grandparents must take seriously. It is a need which we can no longer push to the back burner. Our grandchildren and their children will bear the burden of our irresponsibility in this area. "Once we start to think about the kind of world we are leaving to future generations, we look at things differently; we realize that the world is a gift which we have freely received and must share with others

… the world we have received also belongs to those who will follow us." (*On Care for Our Common Home*, 159).

The pope's concern for the environment and his reminder that grandparents have an obligation to pass the world onto their grandchildren in the best possible condition are not new concepts. Those who have lived close to the earth have lived this wisdom for generations. We have forgotten it now because we live the majority of our lives far away from nature, in more sterile and man-made environments. Native Americans are well-known for teaching care of nature. An ancient Native American proverb teaches: "Treat the earth well: It was not given to you by your parents, it was loaned to you by your children. We do not inherit the earth from our ancestors. We borrow it from our children."

Chief Dan George (d. 1981), chief of the Tsleil-Waututh Nation in British Columbia, Canada, asked grandparents to consider our responsibility in this area: "Have I done all to keep the air fresh? Have I cared enough about the water? Have I left the eagle to soar in freedom? Have I done everything I could to earn my grandchild's fondness?"

Our grandchildren will think of us fondly if we teach them to love and respect nature. If we teach them awe for the beauty of God's creation, they will always have a place where they can go to feel closer to God and to remember us. When we cherish nature, it becomes a part of who we are and who our grandchildren see us to be.

Pope Francis reminds us: "Nature cannot be regarded as something separate from ourselves or as a mere setting in which we live. We are part of nature, included in it and thus in constant interaction with it" (*On Care for Our Common Home*, 139). When we allow nature to be destroyed, we are allowing ourselves to be destroyed. What can we do? We can be more conscious of environmental issues and open to ecological practices we may find initially inconvenient. We can teach our grandchildren to show respect and care for nature. We can pray those who have the power will stop the corruption and destruction.

We are only caretakers, not owners of God's great creation. We must actively work to protect it so one day our grandchildren can share the awe of nature with their grandchildren. "Living our vocation to be protectors of God's handiwork is essential to a life of virtue; it is not an optional or a secondary aspect of our Christian experience" (*On Care for Our Common Home*, 217).

IN AWE OF OTHERS

Perhaps the best-known lover of God's creation is Saint Francis of Assisi. One of his popular prayers/songs is the "Canticle of the Sun." In it, he sings the praises of the sun, the moon, the stars, wind and air, clouds and storms, all other weather, water, fire, fruits and herbs, and colorful flowers. But toward the end of the canticle, Francis switches from being in awe of nature to being in awe of other people. He writes, "Be praised, my Lord, through those who forgive for love of you; through those who endure sickness and trial."

Francis reminds us we can be in awe of much more than nature. People who faithfully live out the lives God calls them to live can also inspire awe in us. Today, people of many faiths are in awe of Pope Francis. The world was in awe of Mother Teresa for many years. The gentle love she showed to the poorest of the poor moved our hearts. We might be in awe of a family member who is extremely patient, a friend who is extremely generous, or a neighbor who is extremely thoughtful. Whenever and wherever we feel awe, we should stop and ask ourselves why we are feeling such an intense or overwhelming emotion. Most likely, we feel closer to God because of this encounter with a place or a person.

For some, our awe is expressed through "the gift of tears." I remember fighting back tears when I saw the Rocky Mountains for the first time. Many of us may have felt close to tears when a grandchild wrapped his or her little hand around our finger for the first time. We cry not only when we are sad or hurt, but also when we experience extreme gratitude, compassion, pride, or joy. These, too, are times of awe. They are moments when God is touching our souls.

For Reflection

1. Do I spend enough time enjoying the beauty of nature with my grandchildren?

2. Are there times in my week when I could find more peace and silence by being alone with God in nature?

3. What steps can I take to protect the environment for the future of my grandchildren? Are there ways I can teach my grandchildren to care for God's creation?

4. Where else in my life do I find awe? Do I feel the glory and goodness of God in a church or cathedral? Who are the people in my life who inspire awe in me? Can I find inspiration in spiritual reading, websites, or videos? Can I share these sources of awe with my grandchildren?

A Grandparent's Prayer

Oh Awesome, Creator God, help me to give my grand-children a great appreciation for the splendor of your creation. Let them always find you in the stillness of the dawn and the beauty of a sunset. Let us together see the glories of nature as "holy ground." Let us walk reverently. Help us treat the world gently — for the sake of grand-children everywhere. Let your Spirit come upon us and renew the face of the earth. Amen.

Chapter 7

Peace

I recently heard a man and woman arguing in a toy store over a birthday gift for their grandson. They stood in front of the video-game section with a list in hand and the grandmother declared, "I am not getting our grandson a violent video game for his birthday!"

Grandpa pointed to the paper and stated, "But it says this is what he wants."

Grandma replied: "He is only seven! He doesn't know what he wants from us."

THE GIFT OF PEACE

It is true. Our grandchildren do not really know what they want from us. They may ask us to run around like crazy in the backyard with them like their friends do, but we may be too old for that. They may hope we will carry them on our shoulders like their daddy does, but we may not be strong enough for that. They may want us to keep up with them on Facebook, but we may not know how to use technology very well. We deprive them of the gifts we can bring to their lives when we try to be someone or something we aren't.

Each grandparent has unique and special gifts to give. Gifts which no one else can. That is what we should offer. One of those gifts can be peace. The world in which our grandchildren live is not a peaceful world. It is rushed. It is noisy and overstimulating. It is stressed and busy. It can be filled with violence and hatred. Family life can be chaotic and stressful even in the best and most caring homes. Society makes it this way, as Pope Francis emphasized in his apostolic exhortation *The Joy of Love*: "Parents come home exhausted, not wanting to talk and many families no longer even share a common meal. Distractions abound, including an addiction to television. This makes it all the more difficult for parents to hand on the faith to their children. [There is] severe stress on families, who often seem more caught up in securing their future than with enjoying the present. This is a broader culture problem, aggravated by fears about steady employment and the future of children" (*Amoris Laetitia*, 50).

While this is all very real, it does not have to be that way in our own homes. A grandparent's house can be a place of peace. We may not be able to change the stress our children encounter in their careers and in their family responsibilities, but we can offer our grandchildren a calm haven.

When I was a new grandmother, I greatly cherished the time to rock and cuddle my sleeping grandchildren. I could hold my granddaughter for an hour, just gazing into her small peacefully sleeping face. When I was a mom, I had a sampler on the wall of our children's room. It said: "Cooking and cleaning can wait 'til tomorrow. I'm rocking my baby and babies don't keep."

It was a nice sentiment, but as a busy mom I rarely followed that advice. Babies were to sleep in their beds, not in your arms. And mothers often need to use available quiet time for getting work done. Now as a grandmother I want to make sure to cherish the peaceful moments. I know they will not last. I also want to give my grandchildren a peace the world cannot offer. Where to start?

GO TO GOD

We cannot give something which we ourselves do not have. If we do not have peace in our own hearts, we cannot give this beautiful gift to our grandchildren. For the sake of our grandchildren, now is a time in our lives when we should be working to cultivate greater peace in our souls. We know where we must go. Jesus is the giver of peace. "Peace I leave with you; my peace I give to you. Not as the world gives do I give it to you" (Jn 14:27).

Throughout our lives we have discovered that material possessions, accomplishments, other people, and even dreams-come-true cannot give us lasting peace, as the *U.S. Catholic Catechism for Adults* explains: "Only in God will we find the truth, peace, and happiness for which we never stop searching. Created in God's image, we are called to know and love the Lord" (7).

Peace is one of the twelve fruits of the Holy Spirit. We receive the gifts of the Holy Spirit when we are confirmed. However, the fruits require our cooperation; they need to be carefully cultivated and nurtured if we want them to flourish in our hearts. Spending more time with God can help us cultivate peace. We might want to consider adding a new spiritual practice with the purpose of bringing peace into our lives, which we can then pass on to our grandchildren. Morning prayer, reading Scripture, daily Mass, Eucharistic Adoration, meditative or contemplative prayer, and spiritual reading are all ways to grow peace in our lives. By spending time with Jesus we can find the peace our grandchildren will want and need from us.

KNOW THE PEACE PRAYER

Most of us have seen or heard the Peace Prayer of Saint Francis — "Lord, make me an instrument of your peace ..." It is possibly one of the most popular prayers of our time. Many people hang this prayer over their desk or carry it in their wallet. Whether or not Saint Francis actually wrote the prayer himself, it reflects the virtues and attitudes he exhibited in living an extraordinary life of peace. If we want to have more peace in our lives, this prayer is a great resource. Consider making it part of your life by committing it to memory.

When we put a prayer someplace where we hope to see it every day, we soon stop seeing it. It just becomes part of the background of our lives — one more thing on the refrigerator, bulletin board, or in our Bible. We don't even notice it anymore. But when we memorize something, we own it. A few years ago, I spent a couple days working to memorize this prayer. Although it had been years since I memorized something, it was easier than I thought it would be. When we memorize the Peace Prayer, we can say it whenever we feel the need for peace — while stuck in a traffic jam, sitting with a loved one in a doctor's office, or even while rocking a crabby grandchild to sleep.

This wonderful prayer seems to cover every situation which causes us stress in our lives and robs us of our own peace. It reminds us in many ways to be forgiving, understanding, and compassionate. It helps us to be joyful instead of stressed, hopeful instead of negative, and giving instead of selfish. It shows us how to eliminate the negatives that can rob our hearts of peace. When we really work on the virtues in this prayer, we gradually find ourselves becoming an instrument of peace in the lives of others — including our grandchildren's.

A PLACE OF PEACE

Mother Teresa, winner of the Noble Peace Prize and a saint who understood the stress of modern times, encouraged us, "More and more make your homes places of love and peace." Young families may have difficulty following that directive, but grandparents should certainly strive to follow that advice. It is not easy. Our grandchildren may resist us, especially as they get older. Routines that might become natural to children in busy or chaotic households do not have to be the norm in a grandparent's home. Activities that keep a child happy while a busy parent is trying to get something done may not be as necessary if grandparents have the time to give their grandchildren personal attention.

Whenever or however possible, we should try to make our time with our grandchildren as peaceful as possible. Let them learn to see us as an oasis of calm in their busy lives. We can offer them simple and quiet activities rather than overstimulating ones. Save the amusement parks for others and take them for a walk or fishing instead. Enjoy puzzles and books with them more than electronic toys. When they are visiting, we might want to eliminate the background noise of television — especially news shows, violent movies, and shopping networks.

Through the beatitudes Jesus taught, "Blessed are the peacemakers, / for they will be called children of God" (Mt 5:9). Let us try to be peacemakers for our grandchildren. It will make them — and us — children of God.

This might mean letting go of expectations, which can cause so much stress in our lives. The more we want everything to be perfect, the more we rob ourselves and others of peace. The perfect family gatherings we see online and in magazines are posed, not real. When we have grandchildren, we may need to give up the fancy dishes for paper plates — at least until they are a little older. We may have to plan dinners that cater more to the needs of the children than to our own tastes. One grandmother of nine says their best family get-togethers revolve around lots of pizza with everyone's favorite toppings. One-dish meals of chili, soup, or stew simmering in a crockpot allow more time to actually be with our grandchildren than in the kitchen. And ice-cream sundaes make a simple yet favorite dessert. Despite what many magazines might try to sell us, family time is not all about the food; it is about the fun. If preparing meals is a source of stress rather than joy, let it go. Choose peace instead. This is a lesson I have personally had to learn many times. It is worth giving up some things in order to have peace.

HAVE ONE-ON-ONE TIME

My grandmother lived very close to the high school I attended. On days when my mother could not pick me up on time, I would walk to my grandmother's house. How I loved those days! I had never been particularly close to my grandmother. She had thirty-seven grandchildren, and I was somewhere in the middle. I did not get to spend much quality time with her. Because I was also the oldest of six children, my own home was never very quiet. When I came into my grandmother's house it was always peaceful and quiet. There was no glare from the sun. The blinds were closed to protect the furniture from fading. She usually had a baked treat waiting for me. She would sit at the kitchen table and talk with me, asking questions and showing an interest in things other people rarely thought to ask about. Those were special times of grace and peace for me.

My grandchildren are all two years apart. While the five-year-old wants to paint, the one-year-old wants to explore and pull things out of cabinets and off shelves. There is nothing peaceful about trying to balance those two activities at the same time. Remembering the peace I found in spending time alone with my grandmother, I strive to schedule time alone with each grandchild so we can enjoy each other at the level most suitable for that child. My oldest granddaughter loves having sleepovers at our house. She nestles on the sofa between her grandpa and me, staying up late, sharing a bowl of popcorn, and watching the movie of her choice without interruptions from her younger brother or sister.

On Sunday morning, she goes to Mass with us. The first time we took her we sat in the back row. I wanted her to be able to stand on the pew so she could see the full splendor of our star-shaped church with its large stained-glass windows. Knowing she loved music, I also wanted her to be able to see the children's choir. As we were singing the *Gloria*, her standing on the pew next to me with our arms wrapped around each other, she whispered in my ear, "Grandma, this is beautiful!" How I hope she will always feel that way about church.

PRAY FOR PEACE

When we think about the world our grandchildren will be inheriting, how can we not want to pray for world peace. Peace in our homes or our small corner of the world is not enough. Mahatma Gandhi, the leader of Indian independence who believed in nonviolent direct action, once said: "Unless one wishes for peace for all life, one cannot wish for peace for oneself. It is a self-evident axiom, like the axioms of Euclid, that one cannot have peace unless there is in one an intense longing for peace all around."

If we want peace in our world, we need to seriously consider the wisdom of these words. Because we are all one family of God, even with those who may not believe or recognize they are God's children, we cannot be at peace in our hearts or our lives if any member of this human family is not at peace. This, of course, is an impossible goal — in real life someone will always be hurting in some way. However, just because we cannot reach the goal does not mean we should give up trying. When we give up striving for more peace in the lives of all people, we start falling backward into less peace. But, when we continue to work for more peace, we can improve our lives and the lives of all those around us.

A great prayer for peace is this excerpt from the prayer Pope Francis offered at Ground Zero when he was in the United States in September 2015. It is particularly appropriate for the threats we face in today's world:

God of peace, bring your peace to our violent world:
peace in the hearts of all men and women
and peace among the nations of the earth.
Turn to your way of love

those whose hearts and minds
are consumed with hatred,
and who justify killing in the name of religion....

Comfort and console us, strengthen us in hope,
and give us the wisdom and courage
to work tirelessly for a world
where true peace and love reign
among nations and in the hearts of all.

We may also want to offer prayers for peace for our grandchildren. At every Eucharistic celebration, we turn to those around us and extend some sign of peace. We don't have to be at Mass to do the same for our grandchildren. They need not even know we are doing it. When we welcome them with a hug, we can do it a little more gently. When we rock them in our arms, we can plant a special kiss on their foreheads. When we hold hands while walking, we can give their little hand a small squeeze. When they drive away in their first car, we can extend our hand in blessing (they will think we are just waving). And with each of these gestures we can softly say, "Peace be with you, dear one." Or we can use the words Saint Francis of Assisi would often use to greet and bless others: "God give you peace." It is a quick but powerful prayer.

"There is an appointed time ... for every affair under the heavens" (Eccl 3:1). Let us believe that now, at this stage of our lives, is "a time for peace" (Eccl 3:8).

By the way, remember those grandparents arguing about the violent video game? I happened to be behind them in the check-out lane. They were buying some classic board games. I hope their grandson appreciated the gift of peace they were offering.

For Reflection

1. Did my grandparents give me a sense of peace? What can I learn from the peace or lack of it that I found in my relationship with my grandparents?

2. Is there an activity I can give up so I have time for a spiritual practice that will bring more peace into my life?

3. Do I have peace in my heart? If not, what one action mentioned in the Peace Prayer of Saint Francis would help me find more peace for the sake of my grandchildren?

4. How can I make my time with my grandchildren more peaceful?

A Grandparent's Prayer

Dear Jesus, Great Prince of Peace, please bless my grandchildren with peace. May the times we spend together be times of peace and joy. May they learn from my example how to value peace, quiet, and simplicity in a world which is often violent, noisy, and hectic. May they know you as the true source of all peace. Protect them from every evil and let your peace reign in their souls throughout their lives. Amen.

Chapter 8

Courage

When my granddaughter turned four, her parents asked her how she wanted to celebrate her birthday. She said she wanted to bungee jump at the mall. For this carnival-like attraction, set up in an open atrium, she barely made the height requirement. People stopped and stared at this little girl flying and giggling like crazy. Afterward, I asked her if she was scared. Her reply was, "Grandma, I thought I could be scared and have no fun; or I could be brave and have fun."

"Be brave and have fun, became a motto in our family. My niece's girlfriends even had a coffee mug and wall hanging made for her with those words. I told my son he might think it was a great motto now for his little girl. However, he was probably not going to like it as much when she turned sixteen.

BEING FEARLESS

I think my granddaughter was born fearless. At three she loved to climb to the top of the very highest slides on the playground, completely unintimidated by the older kids surrounding her. I asked why she had to climb so high. She responded, "The view is better."

She is not intimidated by heights, speed, or other potentially harmful activities. Jump off a diving board? She was doing it at four. Race her scooter down the hill faster than older kids? Not a problem. She is just like her father; scrapes and bruises never bothered him much either.

All of us are fearless in some areas and totally intimidated in others. One person gets stage fright; another can speak in front of a crowd with no problems. One person can hike to the highest mountaintop; another does not feel comfortable walking out onto a second-story balcony.

My granddaughter is certainly not fearless in all areas. She is learning there is evil in the world. She knows some people can be cruel; bad things can happen. She does not like storms, strangers, or being left alone. Yet her fearlessness can still be inspirational. How great would the view of our lives be if we were willing to climb a little higher? How much joy and happiness do we deny ourselves and others because we are not brave?

FEAR NOT

My granddaughter's reflection on her bungee jump contained great wisdom. "I thought I could be scared," she said, "or I thought I could be brave." Courage is not a natural trait. It is a brave choice. Being fearless, however, is not the same as having courage. Nelson Mandela once said, "I learned that courage was not the absence of fear but the triumph over it. The brave man is not he who does not feel afraid but he who conquers that fear."

God knew conquering our fear would not be easy. His commands to "be not afraid" or to "fear not" are peppered more than three hundred times throughout sacred Scripture. He spoke those words to prophets, leaders, and ordinary people. In essence, the message is always the same: "Do not fear nor be dismayed, for the LORD, your God, is with you wherever you go" (Jos 1:9).

In the New Testament, the shepherds were encouraged to set aside their fear and go see the newborn Messiah: "The angel said to them, "Do not be afraid; for behold, I proclaim to you good news of great joy that will be for all the people" (Lk 2:10). Jesus often told his disciples they must choose courage: "At once [Jesus] spoke to them, 'Take courage, it is I; do not be afraid'" (Mt 14:27).

At the Last Supper, Our Lord said: "Behold, the hour is coming and has arrived when each of you will be scattered to his own home and you will leave me alone. But I am not alone, because the Father is with me. I have told you this so that you might have peace in me. In the world you will have trouble, but take courage, I have conquered the world" (Jn 16:32–33). He spoke those words not only for his apostles, but for all of us who strive to follow Jesus in a troubled world.

Despite the many sacred encouragements for us to move forward with courage, we are still reluctant. We hold back, even though wonderful things often resulted when people were not afraid. Battles were won. Shepherds met the heavenly King. The disciples came to see Jesus as God. All this and more can happen when we set aside our fears and embrace the courage God wants us to have.

As grandparents, we will be challenged often to be brave and venture into new waters for the sake of our grandchildren. My father-in-law never got on a plane until his daughter and grandchildren relocated to another state. Then he gave up his fears and became a frequent flyer. My mother was afraid to use e-mail until she discovered it was the best way to communicate with her out-of-town granddaughters. My niece had to finally tell her: "Grandma, stop typing in all caps. It is like you are yelling at me." How many of us have bravely learned new technology such as Skype, Facebook, or the iPhone, just so we could stay in touch with our grandchildren?

The more we wisely take courageous steps, the more joy we may find waiting around a corner for us.

KNOWING WHAT'S RIGHT

Courage, however, is more than just being able to do something new or scary. It is primarily doing the right thing. The Church recognizes courage, also sometimes called fortitude, as one of the cardinal virtues and one of the gifts of the Holy Spirit. It is the strength to do the right thing despite any kind of fear. We receive this spiritual courage from the Holy Spirit at baptism and confirmation. Yet, we can ask the Holy Spirit for this gift anytime we feel we need it. We can also ask the Holy Spirit to shower this gift upon our grandchildren. As they face a future where God and religion may be pushed more and more into the background, it is a virtue they will surely need.

In our society today, it is often difficult to know what is the right thing. More and more shades of gray continue to be added into moral and social issues. While the media may cause us to question many different issues, in our hearts we all know what is right. Pope Francis tells us in his apostolic exhortation *Evangelii Gaud-*

ium, "God furnishes the totality of the faithful with an instinct of faith — *sensus fidei* — which helps them to discern what is truly of God" (*The Joy of the Gospel*, 119). We do not have to have theology, law, or philosophy degrees to know what is right. Even the poorest of the poor and those who are uneducated have planted in their hearts the sense of what God wants from and for all people. For this reason, Pope Francis encourages us to be connected with the poor because "they have much to teach us. Not only do they share in the *sensus fidei*, but in their difficulties they know the suffering of Christ. We need to let ourselves be evangelized by them" (*The Joy of the Gospel*, 198).

What exactly is this "*sensus fidei*" of which Pope Francis speaks? *Sensus fidei*, or sense of the faithful, is the belief that the Holy Spirit instills in all those who are faithful to the Gospel "an instinct for the truth of the Gospel, which enables them to recognize and endorse authentic Christian doctrine and practice, and to reject what is false" (2014 International Theological Commission Study).

This *sensus fidei* is not something that just springs up in the minds of the faithful. In fact, in today's world, where so many unfaithful people are trying to impose their ideas of right and wrong on the rest of the world, it is critically important for those who want to have the courage to do the right thing to take time to understand what the right thing actually is. Church teaching tells us the answer is in our heart. The Holy Spirit has planted it there. But we must cultivate it.

Sensus fidei is not simply popular opinion. It is a truth we hear in our hearts when we spend time in prayer, with the Eucharist, in the life of the Church, in Scripture study, in spiritual reading and in-depth considerations of the issues of our day. We will not learn *sensus fidei* from news headlines, popular commentators, secular bloggers, or Facebook. If we want to inspire our grandchildren to live their faith with courage, we should consider what we are doing in our daily lives to increase our own understanding of our faith and the issues we face. Only when we educate ourselves at the feet of Jesus and those who have been inspired by him will we have the information we need to live our lives with courage and to teach our grandchildren to do the same.

TAKING A STEP

As stated before, courage is a choice. It is also an action. Courage that does nothing is not courage. The classic image of the courageous person is the one who is willing to step forward. It might be the volunteer who steps up for a dangerous mission. It might be the student who steps forward to defend a classmate. Courage always requires us to take a step, even if it is only a mental step out of our comfort zone. The discomfort we fear might be physical or emotional. It does not matter. Acting with courage always puts us at risk of being hurt in some way.

At the 2016 World Youth Day in Kraków, Poland, Pope Francis encouraged youths to have this kind of courage: "He [God] demands of us real courage: the courage to be more powerful than evil by loving everyone, even our enemies. People may laugh at you because you believe in the gentle and unassuming power of mercy. But do not be afraid."

In the Gospels, we hear many stories of people who acted with courage to reach out to Jesus. Every person who came to Jesus for healing showed courage. The two blind men who cried out must have been afraid of a crowd they could not even see telling them to be still (see Mt 20:29–34). The four men who climbed a roof to lower their paralyzed friend down into the room where Jesus was teaching must have feared falling, harming their friend, and anger from the crowd for their "line jumping" (Mk 2:2–11). The tax collector Zacchaeus, who climbed a tree to get a glimpse of Jesus might have also feared falling, anger from the crowd, and rejection from Jesus (Lk 19:1–10). Instead, Jesus called the little man down from the tree, saying, "Come down quickly, for today I must stay at your house" (Lk 19:5). Luke tells us Zacchaeus responded with joy.

That is the wonderful thing about courage. It can turn fear into something good. Joy, accomplishment, peace, forgiveness, fond memories, and love are just some of the many rewards waiting for the one who acts with courage. As my granddaughter discovered, we can have fun in many wonderful ways when we decide to be brave.

For many months, I had been wanting to take my grandson to visit his great-grandfather. Yes, my grandson and my father had met before at family gatherings, but I had never brought them together for a one-on-one visit. In truth, I was a little afraid to do so. My father had been very sick for many months. He could not hear well. He was connected by a long tube to a noisy oxygen condenser. Sometimes he did not have much patience. My three-year-old grandson — like all children — could be unpredictable, fearful, and blunt. I was afraid of what might happen if I brought him to see my father. Yet, I also knew these two people had much in common. They were two of the most special people in my life. And they both loved cars.

The visit was a huge success. I had not seen my dad so happy in months. He loved showing my grandson all of his car-collection memorabilia, and my grandson loved seeing it all. A few weeks later my dad told me his thoughts about the visit. He said when he heard me come in he looked up from his chair and saw a scared little person clinging to my leg. Instantly, my dad forgot about his own aches and pains and tried to make that little boy feel comfortable. The courage my grandson was showing inspired my dad to also move beyond what had been his comfort level over many months of sickness. My dad said it had, indeed, been one of the happiest days he had had in a long time. He told me he hoped I would bring my grandson to visit him more frequently. Then he took me back into a spare bedroom to show me a toy car he had ordered online for all of his great-grandchildren. He wanted his many great-grandchildren to be excited, rather than scared, to come and visit him.

The encounter between my grandson and my father reminds me of the fear we all face at times in drawing closer to God. Like my grandson, we may want to cling to what is comfortable for us and hide our face from a God who seems somehow scary. But God is like a great-grandfather. He wants us to come to him. Our visits with him bring him joy. It is the longing God has for us which inspired Saint Teresa of Calcutta throughout her life. She considered Our Lord's words "I thirst" (Jn 19:28), spoken from the cross, as a longing to have all people drawn to him. Like my dad, who ordered a car online to make his great-grandchildren feel more comfortable with him, God is constantly ordering new experiences and encounters designed to help us feel comfortable visiting with him. We just need to have the courage to see our life experiences as invitations to take another step in our journey toward God.

Courage for today's grandparents requires three steps:

1. We need the courage to draw closer to Jesus than we ever have before in our lives.

2. We need the courage to do whatever God may ask of us as we become one of his closer followers.

3. We need the courage to invite our grandchildren to follow us on this journey.

Once we are truly able to courageously move closer to God in our own lives and follow his teachings more fully, then we will be able to help our grandchildren have that same courage in their lives.

For Reflection

1. Are there areas in my life where I am fearless? Do I see this fearlessness as a gift from God? Do I thank God for this gift and use it to help others?

2. In what areas of my life am I fearful? Have I turned my fears and anxieties over to God, asking him to give me the courage to overcome these fears?

3. Am I confident enough in my beliefs to courageously and lovingly stand up for what I know is right? If I am not confident in my beliefs, what are ways I

can learn to more fully understand what is right and what is wrong in a modern world painted in a thousand shades of gray?

4. What one courageous step is God calling me to take right now in my life so that I can be a better example for my grandchildren? Is God calling me to come closer to him through prayer or study? Is God calling me to live my faith in some courageous new way?

A Grandparent's Prayer

O Holy and Wondrous Spirit, our world greatly needs your great gift of courage right now. Please give me the courage to draw closer to you and to follow your inspiration more fully in my life. Please give my grandchildren the courage to always seek the truth and to stand up for what is right. Please give our world courageous leaders who will work to make a better and safer life for every grandchild born everywhere into this world today. Trusting in your divine power, I courageously place this prayer before you. Amen.

Chapter 9

Generosity

We were walking through a store one day when my granddaughter stopped and exclaimed: "Grandma, my sister would love that shirt! Wouldn't it look cute on her?"

I was impressed with her consideration for her little sister — a little sister who often toddled into her room and messed up her things, wrecked the puzzle she was putting together, or knocked over her tower of blocks. "Should we get it for her?" I asked.

"Yes!" my granddaughter exclaimed. "And something for my brother, too."

When we got home, she rushed to find gift bags. Once in the giving mode, she spent much of her day with me preparing gifts she would bring home to her family. Like most children, my grandchildren love to give. Playing with my old gift bags is a fun activity for them. They love to wrap items in tissue paper, cover them with tape, and then excitedly give the gift. Our responses can help cultivate this natural tendency toward generosity in our grandchildren.

NEVER TOO YOUNG

Children are never too young to give. In our parish, the cash and envelopes given during the collection are put in a large basket. When the gift bearers bring the bread and wine to the altar for the offertory, an usher carries this basket of contributions, placing it at the foot of the altar. This gesture symbolically unites our sacrifices with the sacrifice being made on the altar. One of our ushers is a grandfather who has brought his young grandson to Mass with him every Sunday. When it was this man's turn to carry the basket of gifts, he let his small grandson hold one handle of the basket so they could carry it together. Slowly the young boy has grown to be big enough to wrap his arms around the large basket. Now he can carry it down the aisle by himself.

Children are not mentioned often in Scripture, but when they are, the lessons are powerful. One of the most compelling Gospel stories concerns the multiplication of the loaves and fishes. This is the most frequently repeated story in the Gospels. All four Evangelists write of this miraculous feeding of thousands at least once; Matthew and Mark tell it twice (see Mt 14:13–21; Mt 15:32–39; Mk 6:34–44; Mk 8:1–10; Lk 9:10–17; Jn 6:1–15). The details change in each version, but the story is basically the same. A tired and hungry crowd surrounds Jesus. Our Lord wants to feed them. The apostles tell Jesus there is no food. At this point the stories diverge. Only in the Gospel of John is a child involved. The apostles report to Jesus, "There is a boy here who has five barley loaves and two fish" (Jn 6:9). Jesus does not say let the child keep his food, that he is too young to give. Instead, Jesus takes the loaves and fish from the young boy and feeds five thousand people. Even a child's generosity is, in fact, capable of fueling a miracle.

BRING WHAT YOU HAVE

The other five versions of the loaves and fishes story give us a powerful message on generosity for adults. The apostles complain. They beg Jesus to dismiss the crowds. They say it is impossible for anyone to feed all these people.

Jesus, however, is not concerned. He asks the apostles what they have. "They said to him, 'Five loaves and two fish are all we have here.' Then he said, 'Bring them here to me'" (Mt 14:17–18). That is the same thing Jesus asks of us today — bring him what we have. Through this frequently repeated Gospel story, Jesus is talking to each of us, right here, right now. He is looking us in the eye. He is calling us by name. He is searching our hearts. And he is telling us to bring what we have, no matter how small or insignificant it might seem. He can make miracles happen with it. He told the apostles, "Give them some food yourselves" (Lk 9:13). It is what he tells us to do, too. He shows us amazing things can happen when we are generous. It is also the same thing Jesus will call our grandchildren to do, both now and in the future. The stories have not changed in two thousand years.

Teaching our grandchildren to give and teaching them to be generous are two different things. The boy on the ancient shore of Galilee was not just giving; he was being most generous. Generosity involves making a sacrifice, giving what might be difficult to give. Generosity is giving the last loaf of bread and last piece of fish we have in our baskets. It is not the amount of the gift that makes it generous: it is the amount of the sacrifice. It is possible to give a very large amount without really being generous.

Likewise, the most generous gift might just be a few coins dropped in the offertory basket by a homeless person. This is the message Jesus tried to teach us when he praised the giving of the widow's mite.

Saint Mark tells us, Jesus "sat down opposite the treasury and observed how the crowd put money into the treasury. Many rich people put in large sums. A poor widow also came and put in two small coins worth a few cents. Calling his disciples to himself, he said to them, 'Amen, I say to you, this poor widow put in more than all the other contributors to the treasury. For they have all contributed from their surplus wealth, but she, from her poverty, has contributed all she had, her whole livelihood'" (Mk 12:41–44). If Jesus watched how people gave so long ago in Jerusalem, he probably still watches how we give today.

Generous people do not look around expecting someone else to give. In today's world, too many of us look to others who appear to have finer clothes, a nicer house, or a better job and think, let them give first. We do not look to those who have less than we do and realize we have been blessed with enough to share. No matter how much or how little we have, God has given each of us enough to give something of who we are and what we have to others. This is a message we must teach our grandchildren.

NEVER TOO OLD

Just as we are never too young to learn generosity, we are also never too old to practice it. There is a story about a young man who went to visit his grandfather. You may have heard it before. The old man lived on a large piece of property which was getting more and more difficult for him to manage. The family was planning to move the man into a small retirement community in town. Yet, when the grandson arrived at his grandfather's home, the young man found the old man out in the back, planting apple trees. Worried that his grandfather was in denial about the upcoming move away from the land, the grandson asked his grandfather what he was doing.

"Son," the grandfather replied, "all my life I have eaten the fruit from trees other people have planted. I need to plant some trees from which your children can eat."

When we are generous, we are investing in the future for our grandchildren and even for their children. Generous people give what they have now, no matter how meager or insufficient it may seem to be. They believe God can make miracles with whatever they are able to give. The more we can release even small amounts over to God, the more we will be able to eventually release everything to God. This is true generosity. This is what Jesus calls us all to do.

POOR IN SPIRIT

One of Our Lord's most powerful teachings is the beatitudes. The *U.S. Catholic Catechism for Adults* calls the beatitudes "fundamental attitudes and virtues for living as a faithful disciple" (505). The first of those beatitudes is "Blessed are the poor in spirit, / for theirs is the kingdom of heaven" (Mt 5:3). What does it mean to be poor in spirit?

Being poor in spirit is simply realizing our need for God. It means acknowledging everything we have is a gift from God. We can take credit for nothing. Like the servants who were left in charge of their master's finances in the parable of the talents (see Mt 25:14–30), we will someday be asked by God to show what good we did with the gifts he entrusted to our care. He will not be looking to see how up-to-date our home, wardrobe, car, or technology might be. He will be looking to see how generous we have been.

It is easier to be generous when we think of everything we have as belonging to God. Our task is to no longer consider what we want first, but what God wants. Certainly, God wants us to take care of our own basic needs and the needs of our families. After we do that, however, we need to hear what God is calling us to do with any resources we have left. Those resources aren't just monetary, but can include time, experience, or expertise. Many people think they will give back to God when they have fulfilled all their own wants for good living and financial security. In this world, our list of wants is often endless and keeps growing longer every day. Most of us will never reach a place where we think we have enough. But if we are truly poor in spirit, we will see things differently. We will be able to tell the difference between needs and wants and realize that we do not need nor deserve every comfort or luxury we see advertised or enjoyed by others. Real generosity comes when we give to God before — not after — we indulge our wants.

Real generosity is difficult because today's secular society trains us to be consumers rather than givers. Every day we see and hear endless messages tempting us to buy more and newer things. It is difficult to hear Our Lord's call to be generous amid all this commercial noise. This is why it is so important to cultivate this virtue in our lives and in the lives of our grandchildren. According to Pope Francis, "Humanity will be worse for every selfish choice we make" (*The Joy of the Gospel*, 87).

Selfishness and greed are opposed to being generous or poor in spirit. When we are selfish, we put ourselves and our wants before our genuine needs and the needs of others. Taken to the extreme, we can end up living in a way that is anything but generous. We convince ourselves we need to update our homes before we do anything to provide clean and safe shelter for those living in streets, gutters, and slums, or feel that we are entitled to gourmet beverages when others do not even have access to clean water. When we think of generosity as something that deprives us of the luxuries we want, we can see it as a great burden. But when we are poor in spirit, we realize that all the luxuries and upgrades sold to us are not necessities.

For the poor in spirit, generosity is not a burden; it is a gift. With this approach, we know that we are privileged to have the blessings God has showered upon us and see caring for the poor and needy of this world as an honor. We hold our gifts in open hands, sharing everything we have from God with all his beloved people. The Book of Sirach wisely tells us, "Do not let your hand be open to receive, / but clenched when it is time to give" (4:31).

It is said the best way to let go of something is to never grab hold of it in the first place. This is a powerful reason to introduce generosity to our grandchildren when they are young. The sooner we learn to see everything as a gift from God and not as something we are entitled to, or deserve, the easier it will be for us to be joyfully generous throughout our lives. Even when we do earn money through hard work, dedication, or creativity, we should realize we are only able to earn that money because of the talents, skills, strengths, and education God made available to us. Multimillionaire J. D. Rockefeller reputedly said, "I never would have been able to tithe the first million dollars I made if I had not tithed my first salary, which was $1.50 per week."

Let us teach our grandchildren the virtue of generosity while they are young. It is not hard to do. Despite all the expensive toys with batteries, lights, and music available, a child's needs are simple. My grandchildren's favorite toys were often simple things — a plastic jar full of old spice-jar lids dug from our recycle bin, a colorful set of throwaway cups from a local restaurant, old Christmas cards, stickers sent for free in the mail. We have actually had to "teach" them to play with the larger more expensive toys by coaxing them to try all the buttons and dance to the clanging music. It is cute when they are young. It's not so cute if the message they receive as they get older is to dance to the clanging music of today's consumerism and materialism.

Instead of teaching our grandchildren to want more, let us encourage them to give more. Sometimes the results may be surprising. One beautiful, mild winter's day when I was driving my granddaughter to our house, she noticed all the families out on our street. Everyone was taking advantage of this respite from a cold and harsh winter.

"Grandma," my granddaughter said to me, "I did not know you had kids living on your street. I have to give them something."

When we got in the house, she asked to have her crayons and coloring books. While I worked at putting away groceries and starting dinner, she sat at the kitchen table coloring and chatting with me nonstop. As she finished a picture she would ask me to tear it from the book. Soon she had quite a stack of colored pictures folded in front of her, each with I ♥ U written on the front. Finally, she climbed down from her chair and declared she was finished. It was time for us to go.

"Where are we going?" I asked her, completely forgetting her desire to give something to all the children on our street.

"We have to go give all these pictures to the kids who live here," she said. "I made them for them." She wanted to knock on every door and deliver her special gift. I suppose I could have talked her out of it, but I did not want to discourage this spirit of generosity. However, because it was getting cold and dark and close to dinner time, I convinced her to put one picture in every mailbox. As she skipped along beside me, she expressed enthusiasm about how surprised and happy everyone would be to receive her gift. Yes, I suppose they would be surprised. But the happiest one of all was surely my granddaughter, who was enjoying giving so much. May our grandchildren never lose the joy of generosity.

For Reflection

1. How do I feel about teaching my grandchildren to be generous? Do I see giving as a joyful and blessed experience we can share, or as something children are too young to do?

2. Am I willing to bring what I have to God and others? If I feel that I do not have enough to be generous, why is that? Are there non-monetary ways I can be generous?

3. Sometimes we give to support an organization or activity from which we directly benefit. Am I also giving in some way to benefit people I will never know — nearby, distant, or yet to be born?

4. Am I poor in spirit? Do I give God all the credit for everything I have and own? Since everything belongs to God, do I take time each day to ask him what he wants me to do with the blessings he has given me?

A Grandparent's Prayer

Dear Jesus, knowing you can work great miracles with every gift, I ask you to help me be generous with the blessings you have showered down upon me. Please help me to see and respond to the needs of others, especially those you place in my path. Guide me in encouraging my grandchildren to be generous. Let us together find more joy in giving than in having. I thank you, dearest Lord, for everything and hold my gifts in open hands raised to you. Amen.

Chapter 10

Contentment

It was my granddaughter's first day of school. I had taken my grandson for the day so he would not miss her too much. We had done some shopping, and he picked out a little puzzle for her. It was one of those puzzles you can color with Magic Markers after you put it together. Later in the day, I took him home just in time for bed. His sister, however, was too excited about her new puzzle. She wanted to make it and color it right away. Her mother suggested she should wait until tomorrow because she had already had her bath.

Suddenly, the dam of bravery and acceptance she had been holding back since Mommy and Daddy left her in a strange classroom that morning broke. She began crying. Between sobs, she wailed, "But tomorrow I have school again, and now I will never have enough time to do the stuff I want."

I thought, "Welcome to the rest of your life, dear one!"

KNOW WHEN ENOUGH IS ENOUGH

By the time we have lived to see our children's children, we know a lot about "enough." We know we may never have enough time to do all the things we want. We may never have enough money or enough accomplishments and experiences. And we may never have enough possessions. Yet, if we can be satisfied with what we do have and learn to see it as "enough," we will be content.

Contentment is defined, quite simply, as the state of being satisfied. We can be content if we are satisfied with what we have accomplished, who we are today, and what we have. For many of us, it may take a lifetime to know contentment. Wouldn't it be great if we could teach our grandchildren to be content sooner, rather than later, in their lives?

Contentment is one of the best feelings in the world. It wraps up peace, gratitude, and joy all in one beautiful package. It is a gift we surely want to give our grandchildren. Yet, if we do not have it ourselves, it will be impossible for us to show our grandchildren the way to find it. So how do we find contentment?

Beloved Psalm 23 is a psalm of contentment. It's well-known first verse says, "The LORD is my shepherd; / there is nothing I lack." Other versions of this verse often say, "I shall not want." We hold onto this line as a promise from God. Perhaps, however, it was meant as a command we must follow if we want contentment. If we stop wanting so much and trust God to give us what we need, we will be content.

Even though we may try to stop all our wanting, the secular and commercial world trips us up at every step. The advertising industry specializes in making us feel discontent. Our economy thrives on us being dissatisfied with what we have. We have been trained to always want more. Long before anyone could have imagined how invasive and pervasive advertising would become, the ancient philosopher Socrates stated our fatal flaw: "He who is not contented with what he has, would not be contented with what he would like to have."

No wonder we can't find contentment. We are always looking for something more, new, or different. We no sooner acquire one goal or obtain one possession than we are thinking about what we want next. Instead of rejoicing in the blessings God has given us, we concentrate on the things we do not yet have. This is a foolproof recipe for unhappiness. Yet, we keep running around chasing after the next thing we think we should have.

Saint Augustine gave us an even better reason for our discontent when he wrote: "You have made us for yourself, O Lord. Our heart is restless until it finds its rest in you." Augustine would know. He is a saint who spent a good part of his life chasing after the worldly pleasures of this life.

If we take together the advice of Socrates and Augustine, we will find a path to contentment. We need to realize that more material possessions or accomplishments will never satisfy us. What we need is less "stuff" and more God. So how do we stop craving stuff which just leaves us thirsty for more? For starters, we can stop following the messages which tell us that we are not good enough unless we buy something more. We can disconnect from radio, television, and magazine advertising. We can unsubscribe from the daily sales and bargain messages delivered in e-mail. We can delete apps and tweets which only fuel our longing for something different.

To declare to ourselves and to the world that we have enough is a declaration of freedom. Practicing contentment by choosing to live more simply is not easy, but it can send an important lesson to our grandchildren. It can let them know that God is enough for us; everything else is just window dressing. If they see us putting more attention on the window dressing than on God, what will they think? What will they choose for their own lives?

WANTING LESS

Adam and Eve lost paradise because they wanted something they did not have. Nothing has ever been perfect since, and nothing here on earth ever will be. Having more will not make us happier. In fact, sometimes the more we acquire the unhappier we become. Our possessions fail us. They require maintenance. They sometimes end up owning us more than we own them. Pope Francis frequently warns us of the personal and spiritual risks of wanting and having too much: "Wealth impoverishes us in a bad way" (Apostolic Journey to Cuba, September 2015).

Wealth can, indeed, rob us of contentment. Knowing we can buy something more can cause us to always be looking for something more. I am particularly guilty of this with my grandchildren. I can contentedly say I have all I need for myself. But when it comes to my grandchildren, I always want to give them more. I don't think I am alone in this. We grandparents can be quite good at overdoing it. We love to give to our grandchildren. We may want to do for them what we were not able to do for our own children. Yet, when we "spoil" our grandchildren, we could be setting them up for a lifetime of discontent. We are not doing them any favors. The toy we buy for them may be forgotten on the floor in an hour, but the belief they should always get whatever they want or always receive something more than they already have could haunt them for a lifetime.

If we refrain from overindulgence, we are giving our grandchildren the tools to be content. One important lesson we can teach our grandchildren is the difference between needs and wants. My grandson's favorite outing is to go to the toy store. It can actually be a less expensive outing than taking him to a family-friendly attraction or the movies. He loves to wander through the store and check out all the toys. Sometimes he will tell me, "Grandma, I need this." I always tell him he does not need it; he only wants it. He looks at me and smiles replying, "Grandma, I want this."

We can spend an hour in that toy store. He knows at the end he is only going to get one little toy. He may pick up something and decide he wants it, but as we wander through the aisles he will find something better and run back to put the other item back where he found it. At first, I would become frustrated with the hour of aimlessly wandering through the store. But I realized he was learning important lessons about wanting, having, and needing. Even in the short time he carried a toy around in the store, he often realized it really would not satisfy him. One day, he even surprised me by telling me that he didn't want anything. He just had a good time looking. How blessed we are when we can say we do not need or want any of the endless array of material goods made so readily available in stores and online.

The reality is we will never have all we want in this world. The sooner we accept this the more content we will be. Even if we could have all we want, in the end only God can truly satisfy us. We were made for him. Too much stuff and too many expectations only clutter our lives and rob us of contentment. When we seek to find our happiness in possessions or experiences, we will never be happy, because there will always be one more thing for us to buy or experience. Today, let us be content with what we have.

Our grandchildren will not expect more from us unless we train them to expect more. A friend's story of her nine-year-old grandson's overnight visit verifies this. She had gotten up early to sit in a special corner of her living room and pray. Soon she heard her grandson coming down the stairs. He did not see her hidden in her chair, and she did not interrupt her prayer to call out to him. She heard him wandering around the house, talking to himself about how neat the old house was and how much he liked looking at and remembering all her old knick-knacks and furniture. Our homes, however they are, look like a beloved grandma's and grandpa's house. That is all our grandchildren need from us. That is all we need.

ADMIRE RATHER THAN POSSESS

Just as my grandson can have fun walking through a toy store without buying something, learning how to admire without wanting to possess is another path to contentment. God made a beautiful world, ranging from majestic mountains to delicate butterfly wings. And then he created human beings so we could freely admire and enjoy these splendors. The advertising industry, on the other hand, spends billions of dollars every year trying to convince us we need to possess all we see. Even experiences that were once meant for pure enjoyment — sporting events, family attractions, theme parks — now call us to possess something to remember the experience. Gift shops are often the biggest attraction at places we once attended purely for enjoyment. We need to learn for ourselves, and then teach our grandchildren, how to admire something without having to possess it.

We were driving along an interstate one hot July morning with our grandchildren. Grandpa and Grandma were taking them for a morning walk through a wild bird sanctuary. My granddaughter — always so aware of the beauty of nature — asked me, "Grandma, do you see all those pretty blue flowers by the side of the road?"

I assured her I saw them. Beautiful clusters of wildflowers dotted the sides of the highway, including yellow ones, white ones, and purple ones. But on this day the wild blue ones were most prominent. "Wouldn't it be fun if we could stop the car and pick some?" she hinted.

I agreed it would be fun, but I did not think we could do it. It would be dangerous, it was extremely hot, and it possibly was against the law for us to stop along an interstate to pick wildflowers. Because we are so well trained to be consumers, we can rarely admire without wanting to possess. While the desire to have is rampant in our society today, it is certainly not new.

There is an old fable about a farmer leaning on his fence admiring a bird singing up in a tree. A hunter comes by and the farmer stops him, urging him to listen to the beautiful song of the bird. The farmer marvels at how such lovely music could come from such a tiny creature. He says to the hunter, "I wish I could just have that little bird to hold in my hand." The hunter pulls up his gun, aims, and shoots. The bird falls to the ground. The hunter tips his hat and says, "There you are." Sometimes admiring something is more rewarding than owning it.

Advertising, however, has trained us to see the world as a marketplace where we want to buy everything we see. In contrast, we cannot own the items we see in a museum. We are happy to simply look and admire. We — and our grandchildren — will be more content if we can learn to look at all the world as a museum rather than a marketplace.

A HEAVENLY WAY TO LIVE

Contentment, we could say, is a heavenly way to live. Heaven, after all, will be a place of total and never-ending contentment. Many saints made it through heaven's doors because they knew how to be content here on this earth. They can offer us some wise advice.

Saint Frances de Sales was a busy man. He was a lawyer, theologian, bishop, and writer. He spent much time and energy traveling throughout eastern France and Switzerland during the years that followed the Protestant Reformation. He was fluent in French, Italian, and Latin. He also developed a sign language to teach a deaf man about God. And he founded a religious order for women. He did all of this without the aid of a computer, cellphone, or the speed of modern travel. Yet his advice resonated then and now: "Never be in a hurry; do everything quietly and in a calm spirit. Do not lose your inner peace for anything whatsoever, even if your whole world seems upset."

This busy saint also vowed, "I intend neither to hurry nor to worry." How content might we be if we would take this great saint's advice? What a blessing it would be to not hurry or worry so much?

Saint Teresa of Avila was another busy saint. She is credited with reforming the Carmelite order and starting many new convents throughout Spain. Because of her profound writing, she is one of only four women who have been declared a Doctor of the Church. She, too, taught us contentment comes when we are not attached to so many things: "It is when I possess least that I have the fewest worries."

Saint Teresa encouraged Carmelites to find contentment by teaching them, "If we remember that this house is not to be our home forever, but only for the short period of our life, whatever the length of that may be, everything will become acceptable to us."

Her most powerful message of contentment is one of the prayers for which she is famous: "Let nothing disturb you. Let nothing frighten you. All things are passing away. God never changes. Patience obtains all things. Whoever has God lacks nothing. God alone suffices."

Letting God be the center of our lives surely is a secret to contentment. This is perhaps more important in today's busy and cluttered world than it was in the sixteenth and seventeenth centuries when Teresa of Avila and Francis de Sales lived. Pope Francis tells us, "The emptier a person's heart is, the more he or she needs things to buy, own, and consume" (*On Care for Our Common Home*, 204).

We will be content if we can fill our hearts with God and the good things he has given us. Contrary to what society tries to convince us, a good life does not depend on the material possessions we accumulate or the extravagant experiences we have. Rather, a good life is found in loving relationships with family and friends, in the enjoyment of the natural beauty God has created, and in the satisfaction of helping and serving others. Contentment cannot be manufactured in a factory, bought in a mall, or found online. It is in our hearts, just waiting for us to rest and enjoy it. If we can show our grandchildren this, we will be giving them a gift of immeasurable worth.

For Reflection

1. Saint Paul taught, "Moreover, God is able to make every grace abundant for you, so that in all things, always having all you need, you may have an abundance for every good work" (2 Cor 9:8). Do I believe God has given me enough?

2. In what area of my life do I most need to practice wanting less? Is it material possessions? Is it recognition? Is it excitement and adventure?

3. Am I able to walk through a store, admire the offerings, and walk out, gratefully acknowledging that I do not need anything more than I have?

4. To be content we must slow down enough to enjoy the life we already have. Is there an area in my life where I need to slow down a little more and enjoy the experience of the moment? How can I especially bring more contentment to the time I spend with my grandchildren?

A Grandparent's Prayer

Holy Spirit, please guide and inspire me to be more content with the life I have today, exactly as the heavenly Father has given it to me. Let me enjoy the blessings I have without constantly wanting or expecting more. Help me to show my grandchildren — through my words and my example — how to be content in this life. Let them see the source of true fulfillment is always you and you alone. Fill our hearts with a holy longing for you. Amen.

Chapter 11

Unconditional Love

"If Mommy says no, go ask Grandma." We see these words on baby bibs, gift-shop plaques, magnets, and aprons. They are a great example of a flawed mentality which believes unconditional love means giving a person anything and everything he or she might want. My father was recently the victim of a very common scam aimed at older adults and based on this belief that a grandparent would — and should — do anything for a grandchild.

My dad received a phone call from a young man claiming to be his oldest grandson. The caller said he had been beat up, was in a traffic accident, and now was in jail in a different state and needing money. My dad knew something was wrong. For one thing, any of our children would have turned to my husband and me before they would have bothered their sick grandpa. Instead of falling for the caller's demands, my dad called me to verify my son was safe and nowhere near the scene of the supposed accident. Since then, my dad has received other calls from young people claiming to be his oldest grandson or granddaughter and wanting money from him. Sadly, many grandparents can be taken advantage of in this same way by their own grandchildren who may be tempted to abuse the deep love grandparents have for them.

TOUGH LOVE

Loving deeply and unconditionally often means saying "no." Usually, the hard task of having to say "no" falls to the parents. But as grandparents, we, too, must realize loving a child can often mean disappointing a child — denying them their unrealistic expectations. The truth is that unconditional love is not easy. It is tough. Unconditional love is not giving people everything they want; it is giving them everything they need. Sometimes what a child needs most is discipline, limits, and boundaries. Parents are called upon to deliver that bitter medicine much more often than grandparents. As my mother often told me, and as I have told my own children: "It is easy to raise a brat. It takes a lot of work to raise a well-behaved child." Doing that work is one of the greatest kinds of unconditional love.

Parents are often the ones to do that work. But grandparents, whether we live near or far, are called upon to support that work. Most parents try their hardest and do their best to give their children the unconditional love they need. But, parents live a roller-coaster ride through darling infancy, the terrible twos, loving childhood, and rebellious teen years. Hopefully, the ride ends in responsible and respectable adulthood, but that is not always the case. Most grandparents do not have to go along on that ride. Usually, we do not have to deal with sleepless nights, temper tantrums, impossible expectations, and unacceptable behavior on a regular basis. Thus, while good parenting requires discipline and sometimes tough love, grandparents get to practice what feels like unconditional love to their grandchildren. Many grandchildren do know that if they really want something, it's a good idea to ask Grandma or Grandpa.

As grandparents it is important for us to realize that we just might be blind to the flaws and weaknesses of our grandchildren. If we are not involved in the day-to-day care and discipline, we may not see the challenges the parents face. Whether it is the poor in another country, the pope in Rome, the angels and saints, or God in heaven, the farther away a person is, the easier it may be for us to love him or her. On the other hand, day in and day out closeness makes it easier to more clearly see the flaws in the people we love. And those flaws can start to get in the way of how we show our love. The love is still there, we just may not be able to show it as much as we would like.

God calls us to give love, even when it might be tough: When a Pharisee asked him, "'Teacher, which commandment in the law is the greatest?' He said to him, 'You shall love the Lord, your God, with all your heart, with all your soul, and with all your mind. This is the greatest and the first commandment. The second is like it: You shall love your neighbor as yourself. The whole law and the prophets depend on these two commandments'" (Mt 22:36–40).

NO MATTER WHAT

So how do we follow Our Lord's command? An old proverb says, "Perfect love sometimes does not come until the first grandchild." We could debate for hours the reasons if and why we might be able to love our grandchildren in a way that is easier than any other love. Maybe we are wiser. Maybe they are cuter. Maybe we only see the good in them. Maybe we are not around them enough to get frustrated by them. Whatever the reason, grandparents are generally crazy about their grandchildren. To the point of being down right annoying at times!

Right before my granddaughter started kindergarten, I gave her a little polka-dot dress to wear to school. When she tried it on, I knelt down beside her, hugged her, and told her every time she wore that dress she should remember Grandma loves her very, very much — no matter what.

No matter what happened in her life — when she had a bad day at school, when a friend was mean to her, when she got in trouble — I would still love her.

No matter what happened in my life — if I got sick, if I could not pick her up on a day she was planning on it, if I was out of town or at the hospital with Great-Grandpa — I would still love her.

No matter what she might do — if she was tired and crabby after school, if she did not want to eat the dinner I cooked for her, if she broke something that was mine — I would still love her.

I was not sure if she would remember what I said, but it made me feel good saying it to her. Later that day, I was touched when she finished painting a collection of butterfly magnets and handed one to me. She said, "Grandma, remember when you look at this magnet that I love you very, very much — no matter what."

The key ingredient to this no-matter-what, unconditional kind of loving is forgiveness. It is impossible to love unconditionally unless we are able to forgive. We are all human. We will mess up. We will do the wrong thing or say the wrong thing. We will fail to keep our promises. We will hurt others. The ways we, as humans, can fail one another are innumerable. The only way we can love no matter what is if we are ready to forgive all the little and big ways another person may hurt us. How do we learn that kind of love? By looking at God.

Pope Francis tells us, "If we accept that God's love is unconditional, that the Father's love cannot be bought or sold, then we will become capable of showing boundless love and forgiving others even if they have wronged us" (*The Joy of Love*, 108). When we begin to realize how much we have failed and how much God has forgiven us, then we can start forgiving and loving others. This takes humility and honesty on our part.

Perhaps some of the scariest words in Christianity are the words of the Lord's Prayer, "forgive us our trespasses as we forgive those who trespass against us." Where would we be if God really did forgive us only as well as we forgave? Would he have sent his son to die for us? Would he have promised us everlasting life if he remembered our every little fault and mistake? We can never forgive as well as God forgives, but we must work at it.

The earliest leaders of our Church stressed this forgiveness and unconditional love as a basis for Christianity. Saint Peter taught us, "Above all, let your love for one another be intense, because love covers a multitude of sins" (1 Pt 4:8).

In his beautiful description of love, Saint Paul wrote: "Love is patient, love is kind … it is not quick-tempered, it does not brood over injury.… It bears all things, believes all things, hopes all things, endures all things. Love never fails" (1 Cor 13:4–8).

That is the kind of love we want to teach our grandchildren through our example of loving them and loving others. They can break our favorite coffee mug, rub their little chocolate covered faces on our furniture, or run through our flower gardens. Still, we gently scoop them up and give them a hug. When we show this kind of no-matter-what love and tolerance for our grandchildren we are closer to knowing how God loves us.

My husband hates fingerprints on his car windows. Our children and their friends grew up knowing not to touch the car windows. Not long ago we brought our grandchildren home from an outing. We were standing outside the car talking to my son. The kids were still in their car seats. My granddaughter began to knock on the window to remind us she wanted to get out. My son teased my husband asking why she could touch the car windows which he had never been allowed to touch. My husband laughed and said: "She is my granddaughter. It's different." God says that about us every day.

LORD, I AM NOT WORTHY

Often, we ourselves cannot accept God's unconditional love because we feel unworthy. We may waste a lot of time and energy trying to be worthy of a love for which no person can ever be deserving. God's love is the greatest gift we can receive. We can do nothing to earn it, nor can we do anything to lose it.

Life can get messy when we are not open to receiving God's great love. While we are wasting time trying to earn a love we cannot earn, we may not be doing our best to simply rejoice in the love God gives us. Think of the

Gospel story of Mary sitting at Our Lord's feet and her sister Martha bustling around to prepare the meal (see Lk 10:38–42). Who was enjoying God's great unconditional love more? Martha and Mary are both great saints in our Church, but we cannot forget that Jesus said, "Mary has chosen the better part and it will not be taken from her" (v. 42). Let us strive to choose simple love, to being present with our grandchildren more than endless activity.

When we don't feel worthy of God's love, we may try to fill the emptiness with busyness, material things, and superficial relationships. Saint Augustine lamented the time he wasted not loving God: "Late have I loved you, Beauty so ancient and so new, late have I loved you! Lo, you were within, but I outside, seeking there for you.... You were with me but I was not with you" (*Confessions*, Chapter XXVII). As both Mary of Bethany and Saint Augustine discovered, being with God is the best way to love God.

Today, let us accept that God loved us before we were even born, just as we have loved our grandchildren from the moment we were told they were on their way. Let us realize God loves us with a love much greater than any we can know, even as we love our grandchildren in a way their young and immature hearts do not yet know. My grandson likes to say, "Grandma, I love you." He knows it will usually get a smile out of me and a hug for him. But he does not really know what it means. To our great God, we are like little children. We do not really know what love means. But we can work at learning.

My German cousin tells me we abuse the word "love" in the English language. We use the same word to describe how we feel about a movie or a flavor of ice cream as we use to describe how we feel about our spouse, our children, or our grandchildren. I've wondered if that contributes to why we find it difficult to love unconditionally. We might be unwittingly conditioned by our overuse of the word "love" to withhold our love from a person as easily as we switch our preferences to a different flavor of ice cream or a new movie. We must learn to love like God, who never decides to stop loving us rather fickle people, who love so many things in and out of style every day.

God's love is so powerful and awesome it may even scare us. How do we respond to a God who would die for us? Sometimes when we feel unworthy of a great love, we may push it away or be tempted to deny it. We must be careful not to do that with God. God does not ask us to die for him. He simply asks us to live for him. Living for him means loving all those around us as best we can.

"I THIRST"

When we do question whether we are loving enough or worthy enough, we might consider two of Our Lord's last words on the cross. "I thirst" (Jn 19:28). These words inspired Saint Teresa of Calcutta to leave her comfortable teaching post and go out into the slums to offer unconditional love to the poorest of the poor. She taught us: "Jesus longs for you. He misses you when you don't come close. He thirsts for you. He loves you, always, even when you don't feel worthy."

My husband expressed that kind of longing for our grandchildren one day when I came home from my women's faith group and found him painting our kitchen. When I walked in the door he said to me from the ladder he was standing on, "I miss them."

"Who do you miss?" I asked.

"Those little ones," he answered.

"How can you miss them already?" I asked. "They were just here last night and just left this morning." As we spoke, my son, daughter-in-law, and three grandchildren were driving out of state for a weeklong vacation.

"It's just the idea that there is no way they can pop in anytime this week because they will be too far away," my husband answered.

Oddly enough, at my faith-group meeting, less than an hour earlier, we had been discussing that same kind of longing, or thirsting love. During the discussion, one woman, who had children living out of town said, "I think Our Lord's thirsting for souls is the same kind of longing we feel when our children are gone and you know there is no way you are going to see them for a long time."

Now my husband was saying the same thing to me. It does not matter whether a person has left us for a short time or forever, when we love unconditionally we thirst for them. We look forward to being united with them whenever that might be. When we have a thirsting kind of love, we may start to see our loved one in other people.

Have you noticed as a grandparent you somehow acquire a new love and compassion for all children? I don't remember that happening so much when I was a parent. Maybe it is because, when we are parents, we are overwhelmed with the constant care for our own children. When we are grandparents, we have periods when we do not see our grandchildren and miss them greatly. Thus we see and love them in other children. One grandmother tells of being in a mall with her new granddaughter. She was cuddling the little one while Mommy shopped. A total stranger walked up to her — obviously another grandmother — and said, "Isn't it the most wonderful thing." As the two grandmothers talked, it became obvious this stranger was seeing and loving her own grandchild when she saw my friend cuddling and loving hers. Seeing our grandchildren in other children is a good way to also practice seeing Christ in others.

If we can have a thirsting kind of love for our grandchildren, we can learn how to have that thirsting kind of love for Jesus. We can begin to see him in other people. It is the beginning of unconditional love. It is not easy. In fact, at times it can be nearly impossible. Pope Francis has encouraging words for us on the subject: "None of this, however, is possible without praying to the Holy Spirit for an outpouring of his grace, his supernatural strength, and his spiritual fire, to confirm, direct, and transform our love in every new situation" (*The Joy of Love*, 164).

For Reflection

1. Whom do I find most difficult to love? Why?

2. Having a no-matter-what kind of love requires forgiveness. What do I need to forgive in others? What do I need to forgive in myself? Is there someone I should ask for forgiveness?

3. Am I striving too hard to be worthy of God's love? What do I need to do different in my life to enjoy God's love rather than trying to earn God's love? How can I be a little more like Mary sitting at the feet of Jesus and a little less like Martha scurrying around with activity?

4. How does it make me feel to think that God is longing for my unconditional love?

A Grandparent's Prayer

Dearest Jesus, please teach me to love. Help me to love my family and especially my grandchildren with a no-matter-what kind of love. Lead me to forgive when resentment blocks my loving. May I have the kind of love which inspires my grandchildren to grow into loving adults. May they especially know your great love for them throughout their lives. Amen.

Chapter 12

Trust

We were together at a pool party. My eighteen-month-old grandson had gotten tired of the pool. He was out of his water wings and into dry clothes. But he was having fun playing by the side of the pool, throwing a beach ball to his cousins who were still splashing in the four-foot-deep water. My son, the little guy's daddy, hovered near. He interrupted his conversation repeatedly to step over and warn his young son about getting too close to the pool. In between the warnings, my son set his drink on one of the patio tables. He pulled his cellphone out of his pocket and set it next to the drink. Then he took off his watch and laid it on the table.

Suddenly, there was a splash and a simultaneous scream from a dozen watching mothers and grandmothers. But before most of us could realize what had happened, my son had reached down and pulled his sputtering and crying child from the water. "Didn't I tell you that you would fall in if you were not careful?" my son asked as he gently soothed the child and wrapped him in a towel. My grandson nodded. He had learned two important lessons that day. 1) Listen to his daddy. 2) Trust his daddy.

As grandparents, sitting on the sidelines, we are often blessed to see how our sons and daughters — whether by birth or by marriage — are images of God in the lives of their young children. The way my son warned his son, yet also prepared himself to come to the rescue when the little boy fell into the pool, is a wonderful example of how God works in our lives. God lets us make our own mistakes. Yet he is always ready to snatch us up and comfort us when we fall.

KNOWING GOD

Several years ago, my son and daughter-in-law gave me a beautiful tea set — not a child's tea set, but a set with a bowl-shaped pot and four small bowl-shaped cups. Knowing my love for tea, my daughter-in-law smiled and said, "I thought you might like to have tea parties with your granddaughter."

Thus began a tradition I cherish. Often when I am babysitting we get out the tea set and brew a weak herbal tea. Peppermint has become the favorite. My granddaughter learned quickly to bob the tea bag up and down in the water and carefully lift her little cup to mine and say, "Cheers." As she grew older she wanted to pour the tea, with my hands supporting hers on the teapot. Now, several years later, she is quite adept at hosting the tea party. When she and her siblings visit, they often ask, "Can we have a tea party, Grandma?"

Our tea parties have become a special time for us to just sit around the table, sip some tea, munch on some snacks, and talk about what is going on in our lives. One day when I had the three little ones, the conversation turned to what their daddy and mommy were doing that day. "Daddy's working really hard," my granddaughter informed me. (He was working on a home-improvement project.)

"He be tired," my three-year-old grandson added.

"Maybe he will fall asleep and forget to pick us up," my granddaughter suggested.

"What!" I exclaimed in mock horror.

The kids giggled as they made plans for their imaginary sleepover. They would sleep in their clothes and planned where they would sleep and what they would have for breakfast. Suddenly, my granddaughter put an end to our silly speculation.

"It won't happen," she said, "because Daddy would not go to bed without us. He might fall asleep while he is resting, but then he will wake up and say, 'Hey, where are my kids?' And he will miss us and will get in the car in the middle of the night and drive here to get us."

My granddaughter knew her daddy well. She had an image of him as a man who missed her when she was gone. She saw him as someone who would not rest if she were not safely home. She knew he would get up in the middle of the night to come get her. With that kind of image of her parent it was easy for her to trust him.

What is our image of our God? This is an important question. If we do not have a strong and mighty image of God, we will not be able to trust him. Too often our image of God is not powerful enough. We put God in boxes of our own design and limit how merciful, how wonderful, or how amazing he can be. We need to expand our vision of God before we can expand our trust in God.

Our God is a God so massive he can touch our hearts — all of our hearts together — at one time, with just a figurative finger of his hand, while he reaches out his other hand to touch all the stars in the heavens. Our God is not made of flesh and bones. Although he took the form of a human, he is not a superman trying to fly from one emergency to another and missing some along the way. He is always present to all of us every minute of every day.

To explain the all-encompassing presence of God, Saint Catherine of Sienna used the analogy of God being like the sea, while we are like fish. She wrote, "The fish is in the sea and the sea is in the fish" (*The Dialogue*). This analogy is one way to imagine the words Jesus spoke to his apostles at the Last Supper: "In a little while the world will no longer see me, but you will see me, because I live and you will live. On that day you will realize that I am in my Father and you are in me and I in you" (Jn 14:19–20).

What kind of God is it who can be in us while we are in him? If we were fish, God would surely be the sea. But we live on land. It might help us trust God more if we see him as the air we breathe or the wind that kisses our cheeks.

No matter how some scientists strive to discover or find God, we will never really know him until he is ready to reveal his face to us. But to trust God, we need an image of him we can believe in. Maybe it is the Good Shepherd, who will go out in a storm to find us. Maybe it is a booming voice in a cloud. Maybe it is a broken body on a cross. Maybe it is a miraculous wafer of bread. And maybe it is the air we breathe. When we embrace an image of God that touches our soul, it is easier to trust him more fully.

NEEDING TO CRY

Trusting God will not guarantee our lives will be free from pain, suffering, or sadness. Children soon learn that even the strongest and best parents cannot protect them from everything. But good parents are always there to help carry the burden — no matter what it might be. Likewise, God will not always protect us from misfortune, illness, or even death. The road to heaven always has its rough spots — no matter how much we trust in God.

During another tea-party conversation, my five-year-old granddaughter once confided in me how she dealt with her fears when she was at preschool. "We all get scared when we are away from our family," she wisely declared. "That's why some kids cry. I don't cry. I try to think about other things — like my friends at school or some fun thing we are going to do when I get home with my family again." She tried to share this wisdom with her three-year-old brother who had been crying a lot in preschool. His reply, however, was, "Sometimes I just need to cry."

I found wisdom in this conversation between these youngsters. Even as adults we get scared when we are away from our Father. Yet even when we have developed great faith and trust, sometimes we just might have to cry. Our world will never be perfect.

God has given all of us the same freedom my son gave my grandson when he allowed the little boy to play too close to the edge of the pool despite frequent warnings. The gift of free will means sometimes we will get ourselves into messes. It also means that the free will of other people can cause messes in our lives. So much of the pain, suffering, and violence in our world is the result of bad choices people have made. The bad choices we make do not mean that God is unreliable. God is always trustworthy. He is always there for us. Sometimes, he is even crying tears with us over a situation caused by sin, or by an inclination which left us vulnerable to evil.

Children may think of trust only in terms of strength and protection. The people they trust are the ones who will keep them safe from harm. As adults, we learn that trust also means believing a person will be there for us through good times and bad, to comfort and guide us, or simply to share our burdens. It is important for us to develop this more mature form of trust in God. Some of the many titles of the Holy Spirit include Advocate, Counselor, and Comforter. These are exactly the qualities we would want in our most trustworthy friend. So, wouldn't it make sense to have the divine Advocate, Counselor, and Comforter among our most trusted friends?

Teaching our grandchildren to trust in God is an important part of the faith tradition we want to hand on to them. Yet we cannot teach something we do not know ourselves. Do we trust God enough in our own lives?

UNDERSTANDING TRUST

Some might argue that before we can say we trust God we must know God. But we also must understand trust. Trust is both a verb and a noun. As an action, trust means to believe in the honesty, goodness, virtue, or justice of another person. So, we can ask ourselves: Do we believe God is honest? Do we believe God is good? Do we believe God is virtuous and just? If we believe all these things about God, then we should trust God, even if everything in our lives is not perfect right now. We need to trust that God has a picture of the world, of our future, and of our needs, which is much larger and more complete than any limited vision we may have of what is best for us.

As a noun, trust is defined as a firm belief or a confidence in a person or thing. Think of all the people and things we say we trust. We may have trust in a friend, a blogger, a company, a car, a recipe, or a tool we use. If we can have trust in the people and things we encounter on a daily basis, why do we have trouble having trust in God?

One reason we may have trouble trusting God is distance. Trust is not something we learn from a distance! We usually learn to trust by being closely involved with another person or thing. Only by using a product on a regular basis, working closely with an individual, frequently visiting the same establishment, or spending a good deal of time following a certain blog do we acquire a trust for that person or thing. So, if we do not trust God, maybe the first question we should ask ourselves is if we spend enough time with God?

If we don't spend much time with our amazing and awesome God, we are unlikely to know his gentle and loving ways. If we have not even tried to trust him with the little things, we will be afraid to trust him in a big way. If we are never quiet in the presence of God, we are unlikely to feel the gentle ways he leads and guides us.

God is not loud and pushy. He is subtle. He usually does not shout at us from mountaintops, although he certainly could do that. Instead, he whispers into our hearts in the softest way. We must learn to trust that quiet voice that touches our souls.

Sadly, trust is a virtue which sometimes seems to leak out of us rather than grow stronger as we get older. We may have been disappointed enough by people and situations to feel we can no longer trust completely. People, of course, will disappoint us. Every person is flawed in some way. Every person has the ability to fail us and destroy our trust, and we ourselves have the capacity to damage the trust of others. But we can always trust God.

In recent years, many people have lost trust in both civil and religious leaders because of their immoral and/ or illegal behavior. We have seen throughout history that when civil leaders are no longer trustworthy, injustice increases, wars can break out, and governments can collapse. But throughout history, even when popes and priests have been unworthy of our trust, the Church remains. That is because the Church is the Body and Bride of Christ. I can trust God to be with the Church at all times, even the most challenging ones.

It is important for us to realize that even if God does not answer a prayer as we hope, it is not because he does not care about us or is not worthy of our trust. Perhaps he has a greater plan for us. Maybe he wants us to carry the cross, the disappointment, the illness, or the sadness of our struggle because through it we can grow closer to him or open our lives more to the goodness of other people. Or maybe what we are asking for isn't good for us at all.

Many great people throughout the ages have learned to trust God even in the worst of situations. Abraham, Moses, the prophets, Mary, the apostles, and the martyrs are all people who trusted God, even in great adversity. Look at the life story of any saint and you will see a story of trust. The reward for trusting God may not be earthly gain, but it will be heavenly peace.

STOP WORRYING

Once we are willing to truly hand our lives over to God and trust him to give us all we need, peace will settle into our souls. We can stop worrying. A popular adage says worrying starts where faith stops. If we have true faith and trust in God, we can learn to relax and let God be in charge. I find I sleep better when I hand all my worries over to God right before I go to bed. I trust him to be up all night looking after the people I hold in my heart.

Our Lord was very clear with us on the subject of worry: "Therefore I tell you, do not worry about your life. Can any of you by worrying add a single moment to your life-span?" (Mt 6:25,27).

The wisdom of the Old Testament also encourages people of faith to be people of trust: "Trust in the LORD with all your heart, / on your own intelligence do not rely; / In all your ways be mindful of him, / and he will make straight your paths" (Prv 3:5–6).

Particularly at a time of great tragedy or hardship we will hear people say, "I do not know what I would do without my faith." Personally, I do not ever want to know what I would do without my trust. While cynics may see our trust as a security blanket we need to outgrow, those who believe know trust is the only thing that matters. It is trust in God which makes everything else we do possible. As Pope Francis teaches us, "Basic trust recognizes God's light shining beyond the darkness, like an ember glowing beneath the ashes" (*The Joy of Love*, 114).

Let us pass this beautiful glowing ember onto our grandchildren. When they are filled with worry or anxiety, we can encourage them to say, "I trust you, Jesus."

Many great saints have offered that prayer. Certainly, it can guide and comfort us and our grandchildren.

For Reflection

1. What is my image of God? Do I see him as strong enough and powerful enough to take care of me and my needs? Do I see him as compassionate and loving enough to care?

2. Do I realize that even in bad times I can trust God to be with me — even crying with me? Can I think of a time in my life when God may have cried with me? How does it make me feel to know God cares that deeply for me?

3. When I think of trusting someone or something, what comes to mind? How do I need to improve my relationship with God so that he is the first person I think of when I think of trusting someone?

4. What is one way I could worry less and trust more in God?

A Grandparent's Prayer

Heavenly Father, I know all things are easier when I trust you. Please help trust in you grow strong in my heart. Help me teach my grandchildren to trust in you. May they never hesitate to turn to you with their worries and their needs. Thank you for being such a great and amazing God, powerful and trustworthy beyond my wildest imagination. May I never fail to trust in you. Amen.

Chapter 13

Hope

I have worn a small gold cross around my neck for more than forty years. It was the first gift my husband gave me. I was impressed he chose such a beautiful and simple symbol of my faith. Right after my first grandchild was born, a coworker told me, "Don't stop wearing that cross now that you have a grandchild."

I assured her I wouldn't. I had worn the cross while raising our four children. My friend pulled out a cross around her own neck and told me she had always worn it, too. Although her grandchildren were now in their teens, she told me how her granddaughter, when she was barely a year old, used to love to play with the cross and would search for it if it was buried under a blouse or sweater. Then the little girl's family was transferred overseas. This was in the pre-Skype era, so it was over a year before my friend saw her little granddaughter again. When the family returned for a visit, she eagerly waited to greet them at the airport. The now two-year-old grandchild was shy and afraid of the grandmother she had not seen for so long. My friend had an idea. She reached around her neck, found the cross and, with a smile, held it up for the little girl to see. The grandchild hesitated for just a moment, smiled broadly, and reached out her arms to her grandmother.

"I always liked that she knew me by my cross," my friend said. Wouldn't it be wonderful if all our grandchildren would know us by this powerful sign of our faith?

HOPE IN THE CROSS

The cross is a beautiful sign of hope. Once an instrument of great torture, it is now a reminder of the greatest love ever known. Just as Jesus stretched out his arms to be crucified for us, God's arms are always open to embrace and welcome us. Like the prodigal son of the Gospels, who found his father waiting with arms wide open, none of us will ever be turned away from God's great love and mercy. Even a man who had done things terrible enough to warrant being crucified next to Jesus found hope in his cross.

Like the "good thief" who was crucified with Jesus, none of us are too hopeless to be turned away by God. Jesus told the thief, "Amen, I say to you, today you will be with me in Paradise" (Lk 23:43). It is the ultimate hope to which we all cling. To be with Jesus forever in heaven.

In recent years, hope in God's divine mercy has grown because of a poor Polish nun, now known as Saint Faustina. Sister Faustina Kowalska is responsible for spreading the message that God wants to be merciful to us. What greater hope can there be than this? She introduced the world to an image of Jesus, Lord of Mercy, robed in white with rays of love radiating from his heart. She encouraged the praying of a Divine Mercy Chaplet and promoted an observance of divine mercy that later became Divine Mercy Sunday, recognized on the first Sunday after Easter. She taught us to set aside the three o'clock hour each day as a special hour of God's mercy. All these practices remind us that God loves us so much he allowed his Son to die on a cross for us. The overwhelming mercy of God is our hope at all times.

Realizing how much our current age needed mercy and hope, Pope Saint John Paul II chose Sister Faustina to be the first saint canonized in the new millennium. Her sainthood was declared on the day that become Divine Mercy Sunday in the year 2000. She is a saint for modern times and a saint for the future. She is one to whom many of us would want to introduce our grandchildren.

HOPE FROM THE PAST

A friend was talking to her grandchildren about something she had done when she was a little girl. Her young grandson was amazed. "Grandma, you mean you were once a little kid like me?" he asked.

"I sure was," Grandma answered. "And I was once a baby like your little sister."

Her grandson shook his head in disbelief. "Wow! I didn't know babies could have white hair."

A child's world is very small. It is difficult for them to imagine things being any different than they are right now. They cannot believe their parents and grandparents were once little children like them. In the same way, we, too, might have a difficult time imagining a life different than the one we have now — a life where we have no more sorrows or aches or pains; a life where we are united with loved ones who have gone ahead of us; a life where we live in the constant joy of God's unending love. However, just because we cannot imagine it does not mean it is not true. As my grandfather used to always tell us, "There is so much you do not know, it is pitiful!"

At some point our grandchildren begin to realize we were not always old men and women. We were once children like them. We were once a mommy or daddy, just like their mommy and daddy. And they will begin to want to hear stories and see pictures from our lives. Pope Francis has said: "Hope is ... nourished by memory; it looks not only to the future but also to the past and present. To keep moving forward in life, in addition to knowing where we want to go, we also need to know who we are and where we come from" (Apostolic Journey to Cuba, September 20, 2015).

Sharing our own life stories with our grandchildren can inspire their future. Let us resolve to tell them stories of faith and hope rather than stories of secularism and materialism. When I became a grandmother, my daughter-in-law gave me a wonderful gift — a journal called "Grandma, Tell Me Your Story." Such a journal is just one way to make sure our grandchildren know the family strength that runs in their veins.

Pope Francis encourages us to tell our grandchildren these stories of our past: "Listening to the elderly tell their stories is good for children and young people; it makes them feel connected to the living history of their families, their neighborhoods, and their country. A family that fails to respect and cherish its grandparents, who are its living memory, is already in decline, whereas a family that remembers has a future" (*The Joy of Love*, 193).

Knowing the road we have traveled — as a people and as a family — gives us the strength to face the road ahead. Hope begins to grow in us when, as children, we realize we will not always be small, that we will not always be dominated by the limitations and schedules imposed on us by others.

My grandchildren love looking at pictures of their daddy when he was little. One of their favorites comes from a time when he was in a high school band with longer hair and a guitar slung over his shoulder. Although they cannot actually verbalize the concept, I think they find hope in knowing their very clean-cut, strong, and powerful dad was once what they call "a silly kid with long hair."

As grandparents, it is important for us to realize the role we play in opening the future before our grandchildren. My dad has no memories of his grandparents. His father came to this country alone at the age of eighteen. His maternal grandfather died before my dad was born and his maternal grandmother died when he was only two. Now that I am a grandmother and telling him stories of my grandchildren, he often tells me how lucky my grandchildren are to have me in their lives. If I am needed to babysit on a day I was planning to spend with him, he always tells me to spend the day with my grandchildren. "They need you," he tells me. He says he always envied his friends who had grandparents who would come to visit for holidays, who snuck a nickel into his friends' hands, or who took them on adventures out into the country.

Through those little gestures we, as grandparents, can offer hope to our grandchildren. As more people question the possibility of a God, our world becomes more hopeless. We can show our grandchildren hope. For many the dawning of each new day is a reason for hope. The same sun which warmed the days and lit the way for our ancestors is shining on us and on our grandchildren. When we remind our grandchildren of this, we offer them hope. Just as the sun is not exhausted, we must remember, "The LORD's acts of mercy are not exhausted,

/ his compassion is not spent; / They are renewed each morning ... / The LORD is my portion, I tell myself, / therefore I will hope in him" (Lam 3:22–24).

BELIEVING IN SOMETHING BIGGER

It is said that one thing which differentiates us from animals is hope. An animal — even a beloved pet who seems to understand sadness or joy or loneliness — does not have hope. Hope — along with faith and charity — is one of the three theological virtues. Only human beings are capable of these virtues, which bring us just a little bit closer to God. Hope allows us to look at the future and believe it will be better — because of God's love, mercy, and goodness. Animals are not able to do this. And when we — as individuals or as society — fail to do this, we become like animals.

Many pet owners consider it inhumane to put their pets through long and painful medical procedures because they know the animal does not understand hope. As humans, we often take this virtue for granted. We can endure suffering because we have hope. We believe the suffering — whether it is as simple as final exams or as intense as months of chemotherapy and radiation treatments — will lead to a good outcome.

Hope is a positive emotion full of promise and expectation. It is joyful anticipation. For our young grandchildren, the best example of hope might be waiting for Santa Claus. Since June, my granddaughter has talked about how Santa Claus might bring her a new bike with only two wheels. She is full of hope at the idea of receiving a big-girl bike. She has told me she must wait for Santa Claus to bring the bike because it is too big for her mommy and daddy to just buy for her. I smiled at the irony; it will be her mommy and daddy who will make this special wish come true.

Sometimes, we think of God in the same way. We refuse to hope because we think the thing we want is too big for God to handle. This is why the Church gives us Advent as a season of hope. During that wondrous time of the year, we are reminded Christ took on our humble human form so he could live among us and personally show us his great love and mercy. Many years ago, I heard a priest suggest a good way to keep the hope of Christmas alive all year.

Before packing away our Nativity sets, we should pick one figure to keep out all year. If we want to be more trusting, we might leave Joseph sitting on our desk. If we want to be humbler, we might leave a shepherd on our mantle. If we want to be more joyous, we can leave an angel sitting on the top of the refrigerator. Some years, I leave Mary, Joseph, the Infant Jesus, and an angel in my kitchen hutch, so I have a visual of the love, trust, peace, and joy of Christmas hope.

The hope of Christmas leads us to the even greater hope of the Resurrection. Because Jesus rose from the dead, we have the hope of eternal life. It is there we will be united in a glorious community with all those we love and with all those who have loved us. It is there we will be able to introduce our grandchildren to our grandparents. It is there all worries, disappointments, sadness, and sin will be washed away in the golden light of God's love. This is a hope we must surely introduce to our grandchildren as they grow and mature.

HOPE IN COMMUNITY

Even when we are surrounded by sacred words, feasts, and icons, it can be difficult to hope alone. My granddaughter became more hopeful about getting her Christmas bike when she shared her hopes with me. The more we talk about our hopes, the more we believe they can come true. Because our true hope is centered in God, it is most important to be connected to people who want to talk about God. Connections with family, friends, neighbors, and members of our church community all help us grow and maintain hope.

The first community in which we experience hope is the family. As Pope Francis tells us, "One of the most important tasks of families is to provide an education in hope" (*The Joy of Love*, 275). As we grow into adults and leave our family community, connecting with our church community can help us learn to place our hope in something much greater than just ourselves. A good place to start is regular Mass attendance. Jesus promised us, "I am the bread of life; whoever comes to me will never hunger, and whoever believes in me will never thirst" (Jn 6:35). Frequent Mass and holy Communion bring us into closer union with this promise of great hope — the wonderful bread of life!

Beyond attending Mass, it can be helpful to become involved in some type of faith-sharing group, Bible study, religious book club, or support group. There we will encounter people carrying burdens much greater than ours but still filled with divine hope. There we will hear stories of God's wonderful work in other lives. There we will be humbled enough to know hope.

An example of sharing hope with a community is how we often come together in the face of a disaster or tragedy. One of the greatest tragedies in our lifetime was 9/11 — something our grandchildren will know only through history books. At that time, we came together as a people of hope. Our churches were full. We prayed together, we worked together. Reflecting on that disaster, the U.S. Conference of Catholic Bishops wrote: "Hope assures us that, with God's grace, we will see our way through.... For believers, hope is not a matter of optimism, but a source for strength and action ... hope is the indispensable virtue" (*A Pastoral Message: Living with Faith and Hope after September 11*).

Those wise words are not just important in the face of overwhelming tragedy; they can guide us throughout our lives. They are something of great value which we must pass on to our grandchildren. Every day someone faces a personal tragedy. Every day someone's life is suddenly shattered. Sadness, heartbreak, and depression surround us. Yet, our hope can see us through even the darkest moment.

We must never forget the beautiful words God spoke to Jeremiah: "For I know well the plans I have in mind for you ... plans for your welfare and not for woe, so as to give you a future of hope" (Jer 29:11). God speaks those words to us. He speaks those words to our grandchildren. We just must listen.

My granddaughter was five years old and just getting interested in wearing jewelry when she paid special attention to the cross around my neck. "Grandma," she said, "every time I see you, you are wearing that cross."

"That's because I wear it every day," I told her.

"Papa wears a cross, too," she stated. "Why do you both wear a cross every day."

"It shows people that we love Jesus," I answered.

"Well, I love Jesus," she said. "Can I wear a cross?"

"You sure can."

"Can I wear it every day?"

"I hope you do," I said.

That is most definitely my hope.

For Reflection

1. Do my grandchildren see me as a person of faith? Will they grow up associating a cross or other symbol of faith with me?

2. Do I tell my grandchildren stories of hope and faith from my past? What story of faith do I still need to tell them? Should I consider writing it down for them?

3. Do I celebrate the holidays in a purely secular way, or do my grandchildren see my hope and faith reflected in the way we celebrate Christmas and Easter?

4. Am I working to cultivate my own hope by sharing my faith with others who can encourage me to believe more fully and more deeply?

A Grandparent's Prayer

Jesus, my Lord, thank you for bringing hope to our world through your life, death, and resurrection. Help me to live and die with hope in your love and mercy. Show me how to pass hope on to my grandchildren. Inspire me to tell them stories which will instill in them both love for you and hope in your promises. Let them live always with hopeful hearts. Amen.

Chapter 14

Joy

My granddaughter discovered joy in stacking blocks when she was sixteen months old. If she saw me get out the bag of blocks, she would run over to me and plop down on the floor, shaking with excitement as she waited for me to open the bag. At first, she was content to reach in the bag and grab out one block after another. Soon she would be tugging at the bag and dumping all the blocks around her. She would grab two blocks and stack them together, then reach for another. Each time the blocks locked together she would smile or giggle with pleasure.

She got very good at stacking the blocks as high as her little arms would reach. Then I would stand her up so she could stack them higher. She never cried when the tower eventually tumbled. She would just plop down on the floor and start stacking again with the same joy she had at the start. She never cared what color block she used next. Sometimes she would start multiple towers at the same time. She had no plan. She had no expectations. And she had no disappointment. She just had joy.

As we get older, the world gets in the way of that kind of carefree joy. Worries and expectations can prevent us from experiencing simple joy in the moment. We begin to realize we need a plan if we are going to accomplish something. This way of looking at things happens sooner than we might suspect. When my granddaughter's older brother plays blocks with her, he knows he wants the red ones to make a garage for his red car and the blue blocks to make a garage for his blue car. He gets upset if he does not have the colors he needs.

In his First Letter to the Thessalonians, Saint Paul gives Christians three important instructions for life: "Rejoice always. Pray without ceasing. In all circumstances give thanks, for this is the will of God for you in Christ Jesus" (5:16–18). If this is the will of God, then it seems these are three important lessons for us to pass on to our grandchildren. In the last three chapters of this book we will look individually at these critical lessons from Saint Paul.

JOY FIRST

I am not surprised my young grandson has a very definite plan for what he wants to build with his blocks. He gets the planning gene from me. Ask me to do something and I start breaking it down into small chunks and slotting those tasks into my calendar. However, the more I plan the less I seem to have joy. After all, you can't make an appointment or schedule a time for joy. Joy can sneak up on us at the most unexpected times. For a dedicated planner like me, joy can even get in the way of the scheduled activity for the hour. But Saint Paul tells us, "Rejoice always" (1 Thes 5:16). How exactly do we do that?

When I was a mother with young children, I once heard the following advice: "Joy is knowing God has a plan; and it is always better than my plan." I wrote that line on sticky notes all over the house. I needed to embrace the idea that God would interrupt my plans all day through my children. And these interruptions could bring me more joy than my own plans ever could!

One of the things I now love about being with my grandchildren is ignoring my planning calendar and to-do list. When I am with them, we do whatever inspires us, and we have a joyful time doing it. Making joyful memories with grandchildren should be a top priority when they are around. Establishing silly and fun traditions is a must. So is staying calm, gentle, and flexible. We blow bubbles. We spread a quilt on the family-room floor for a picnic lunch. We throw tablecloths over the dining-room table to make a tent. We use flashlights to search for the stuffed animals that magically escaped one night from the upstairs toy room to the basement.

It has been said, "If you want to make God laugh, tell him your plans." If God can laugh at our sidetracked plans, then surely we can take joy in setting them aside and doing something more spontaneous. At a recent family Christmas party, I heard a memorable tale of a grandmother's spontaneous gift of joy. My sister had announced a game. Each person had to share a special Christmas memory. The person who shared the best memory would win a prize.

My niece's husband told the winning tale: When he was a young boy, his family tradition was to go to Christmas Eve Mass with his grandparents. The family would then gather at the grandparents' home for dinner and gifts. One year, as they were lingering by the Nativity scene in front of the church, his grandmother whispered in his ear, "You know if you put some of the Christmas hay in your pocket it will turn into money."

He slyly snuck his hand close to the crib and grabbed a few pieces of hay to stick into his pocket. That night, when he retrieved his coat from this grandparents' room, there was money in his pocket where the straw had been. Every year after that, he would stick straw in his pocket on Christmas Eve and his grandmother would replace it with some coins. It was not until his grandmother died that he told the rest of the family about their magical and joyful holiday tradition.

Surely, that young man's grandma had more important things to do than put a few coins in a little boy's coat. She was hosting Christmas Eve dinner for her family. She had last-minute preparations to make, dishes to wash, and guests to entertain. But amid all that she had time to create a bit of joy her grandson would cherish his whole life. Joy is that simple. It is making ordinary moments special in some way.

Joy is a warm contentment that overwhelms us when we know God is in charge. An outdoor church sign once said, "If God is your copilot, change seats." If we let God truly drive our lives — putting him and his plans for us above all else — he will lead us to joy.

SEE THE GOOD

Saint Paul not only told us to always be joyful; but he also told us how to do it: "Rejoice in the Lord always. I shall say it again: rejoice! Whatever is true, whatever is honorable, whatever is just, whatever is pure, whatever is lovely, whatever is gracious, if there is any excellence and if there

is anything worthy of praise, think about these things"
(Phil 4:4,8).

How often do we think about what is good and
lovely in our lives? And how often do we think about
what is lacking or annoying in our lives? Joy comes when
we see how good our lives are. Yet, sadly, most of the time
we are looking at the negative rather than the positive.
Why is that? We can walk into a beautiful room and the
one thing that jumps out at us is the towel on the floor or
the smudge on the wall. We often expect everything to be
perfect in a world that will never be perfect.

Driving out to my son's house for an early morning babysitting session I was looking at the negatives. I
had to get up at 4:00 a.m.; I was tired; the road was dark
and deserted in this early morning hour; my husband
was not able to come with me as he often did, so I knew
juggling three young children alone was going to wear
me out. Suddenly, I was filled with shame at my negative
thinking. What was wrong with me? I was going to get to
spend the morning with my darling grandchildren. Their
faces would light up with joy when they saw me, and they
would run into my arms. We would sit around the breakfast table and catch up on what they had been doing since
I last saw them. The sky was clear with the last morning
stars slipping away and the weather was beautiful. Lovely
music from a Christian radio station was filling my car —
a station which incidentally went by the call letters J-O-Y.
But instead of filling my heart with joy, I had been letting
the negatives crowd out the positives.

If we are going to live as people of joy, it is important for us to follow Saint Paul's advice to always strive to
see the thing that is worthy of praise.

BE GOOD

While Saint Paul told us to look for the good in life, Jesus gave us a more challenging recipe for joy. Our Lord's most important instructions for living a joyful life were delivered to his followers in a sermon on a mountain. Those lessons are called the beatitudes. The *United States Catholic Catechism for Adults* states: "The word Beatitude refers to a state of deep happiness or joy. These Beatitudes are taught by Jesus as the foundation for a life of authentic Christian discipleship and the attainment of ultimate happiness" (308–309).

What are those qualities or actions which will lead us to joy? They are spelled out as part of Matthew's Gospel of the Sermon on the Mount (see Mt 5:3–12). First, we are to be poor in spirit, not getting caught up with material possessions. We are also called to be humble, merciful, clean of heart, and peacemakers. We are to want what is right so passionately that it becomes a hunger or thirst in our hearts. And we are to accept grief and persecution. If all of this sounds a little familiar it is because we have already discussed many of these points in chapters about contentment, generosity, peace, and other virtues we want to share with our grandchildren. The simple fact is that living a life of virtue and faith leads to joy.

Catholic writer and theologian Fr. Henri Nouwen summed it up nicely when he said: "True joy, happiness, and inner peace come from giving of ourselves to others. A happy life is a life for others."

In recent years, that statement has been tested in a series of research projects designed to see what gives us more joy — serving our own needs or helping someone else. Study after study has shown we are happier when we are helping others. In one study, researchers tracked how college students used $50 given to them to either spend on themselves or donate to a favorite charity. In another study, corporate executives were asked how they used their large profit-sharing bonuses. The results were always the same. Those who gave away some or all of what they had received reported more joy and a deeper feeling of satisfaction than those who spent all the money on themselves. If we doubt the findings, we can simply conduct the test ourselves. Do something for someone else and compare the joy that action brings with the joy we get from only taking care of our own needs and wants. It seems we always walk away with a warmer glow and a deeper sense of joy when we have helped someone else — whether a friend, family member, or stranger. The most joyful people are those who serve.

Why is that? One reason may be true joy only comes when we are following God's plan for us. And God's plan is for us to serve one another: "Whoever wishes to be great among you shall be your servant. The Son of Man did not come to be served but to serve" (Mt 20:26,28).

We will discover in life two kinds of dreams. The first are the ones a materialistic society has instilled in our minds. Chasing these dreams may bring momentary happiness, but never deep joy. The second kind of dreams are those God instilled in our souls. Those dreams revolve around sharing ourselves with others as God envisioned when he blessed us in a very special and unique way. Following the dreams of our soul will bring us great joy.

Pope Paul VI is one of many Church leaders and saints who has told us joy comes from doing good. In his apostolic exhortation on Christian joy he wrote: "Joy cannot be dissociated from sharing. In God himself, all is joy because all is giving" (*Gaudete in Domino*).

COME, HOLY SPIRIT

Our guide to knowing how God calls us to give is the Holy Spirit. He has bestowed great gifts upon us so we can do what will bring us joy. Those seven gifts are wisdom, understanding, knowledge, counsel, fortitude, reverence, and awe. When we use these gifts well we get even more gifts, known as the twelve fruits of the Holy Spirit. Those fruits are charity, peace, patience, kindness, goodness, generosity, gentleness, faithfulness, modesty, self-control, chastity, and joy. We may not have thought much about these gifts and fruits since we were confirmed, but they are there for us always. We just must be open to letting the Spirit transform us and work through us.

What all this Church doctrine means in simplest terms is that the Holy Spirit is our guide to joy. If we listen to the promptings of God's amazing Spirit, he will lead us to the right next step for us. Of course, if we are going to follow the Spirit, we must be willing to be spontaneous and flexible. He will throw opportunities for joy at us in the most unexpected and unusual ways. The more we can respond to his promptings — whether they are part of our plan or not — the more we will know joy.

We may not know where the Spirit will lead us next, but we can be sure he will always lead us to Christ, who is the ultimate reason for all joy. Knowing Jesus lived, died, and rose for us can be a constant source of joy for us. In the Middle Ages a custom developed in the Church known as "Easter Laughter." The idea was people should be so joyful because Jesus had risen from the dead that they would break out in laughter. To make sure this happened, priests loaded their Easter sermons with jokes and funny stories.

We, too, should greet each day with a holy joy which comes from knowing God loved us so deeply he sent his Son to live among us. He suffered a horrible death for our salvation, but he does not want us wrapped up in the sadness of that event. He wants us celebrating with joy and sharing in his victory over sin and death. God will always be victorious. Good will always conquer evil. The positive is always better than the negative. For that reason, we can laugh. We can smile. Our lives can sparkle with joy.

A great woman of joy in modern times was Saint Teresa of Calcutta. Despite her own interior struggles, Mother Teresa believed in spreading joy with a smile. She often said, "We shall never know all the good that a simple smile can do." When we have nothing else to give, we can always give a smile. At the canonization ceremony for Mother Teresa, Pope Francis spoke of the way she would spread joy with a simple smile. He reminded us: "Mother Teresa loved to say, 'Perhaps I don't speak their language, but I can smile.' Let us carry her smile in our hearts and give it to those whom we meet along our journey, especially those who suffer. In this way, we will open up opportunities of joy and hope for our many brothers and sisters who are discouraged and who stand in need of understanding and tenderness."

With the help of the Holy Spirit we can give joy to others. We can smile at all those we meet and in every situation. In that way, our own joy will radiate out to others and grow stronger. When we are with our grandchildren, let us always be people of joy. Let us model for them how to spread joy wherever we go.

For Reflection

1. Can I think of a time when I set aside my scheduled plans in order to spontaneously do something joyful for myself or for others? How did that make me feel?

2. We are often people who look for the negative rather than the positive. Can I think of a time when failing to see the good cost me the possibility of joy?

3. Have I had the experience of feeling joy after helping someone? Is it possible for me to know more joy by being more generous to others?

4. Do people see me as a joyful person? How can I let the joy of Christ's resurrection radiate out from me every day of my life?

A Grandparent's Prayer

O Holy Spirit, Great Bringer of Joy, please shower my grandchildren with your fine fruits. Give them the ability to live joyful lives. Let them see in me a witness to the joy that comes from serving others and walking by your guiding light. Help me to release any plans, expectations, fears, or anger that may rob me of joy. Let me be always joyful, especially when I am in the presence of my dear grandchildren. Amen.

Chapter 15

Prayer

My grandson gets prayer. At only three years old, he has been carefully taught to say the prayer before meals. He makes the Sign of the Cross and pronounces words which have no meaning to him: "which we have received through thy bounty." But when we have finished this traditional blessing and are reaching for our forks, he shouts out, "Thank you, God, for this food." These are words he understands.

Prayer absolutely must mean something to us. We should both know and feel the words. In a world as busy as ours, we are not going to make time for anything which has no meaning for us. As noted in the previous chapter, Saint Paul gave us three simple lessons to guide our lives. One of them was, "Pray without ceasing" (1 Thes 5:17). How can we possibly pray without ceasing, or even pray at all, if we find prayer boring or uninspiring? And how can we pass this most important habit on to our grandchildren if we have not made it a constant in our own lives? To begin, we must be comfortable with God.

GETTING COMFORTABLE

Here is a simple reality. We enjoy spending time with people we know. Most people are not very comfortable with strangers. Unless we are seeking political office or trying to sell something, we do not relish the idea of walking into a room and approaching a person we do not know. Instead, we look for a familiar face.

So, is God a familiar face in our lives? Yes, we know his story told through the Gospels. Yes, we recognize his face on every crucifix and in every piece of artwork, although artists around the world depict him in many ways. But do we really know God? How often do we sit down and have a great conversation with him? How often have we been so comfortable with him that we just want to sit in silence with him or feel his arm wrapped around us? If we can build this kind of close relationship with God, then we will know a prayer so rich we will want to pray constantly. It is this kind of prayer we want to teach our grandchildren.

In his autobiographical collection of his journals, *Journal of a Soul*, Pope St. John XXIII wrote of being inspired to pray better when he thought of the story of Jesus coming to Bethany after hearing of the death of Lazarus. Martha runs out to meet Jesus and tells him of her frustration about her brother's death (see Jn 11:20–21). After talking with her, Jesus asks her where Mary is. Martha returns home and tells Mary that Jesus is looking for her. So, Mary runs to him crying (vv. 28–32). It is a story of two women praying in different ways, yet both with sadness and hope. Jesus loved and comforted them both like a true friend would.

If we think of praying as simply talking with God, then the Bible is full of people praying. Every interaction every person in Scripture had with God was a way of praying. The apostles afraid in the boat were praying. The woman at the well arguing with Jesus about giving him a drink was praying. The disciples telling Jesus they had no idea how to feed five thousand people were praying. If we can just learn to turn to Jesus no matter the situation in our lives, we will become masters at praying. Can we picture ourselves, just like Mary, walking arm in arm with Jesus, talking about what we have been doing and what we have been feeling? That is how we are invited to pray!

Of course, gaining that level of confidence with God takes time. It takes being together with God as much as we can in the midst of the daily responsibilities of our vocations. It means taking him along with us no matter where we are going and what we are doing. Ideally, it means having the same kind of relationship with God as we want our grandchildren to have with us.

My family is large. My parents had six children and twenty grandchildren. Now, many of those grandchildren are married and having children of their own. When we gather together, as we did a few years ago for my dad's eighty-seventh birthday, it becomes quite a crowd. When my son and daughter-in-law walked into this group with my three-year-old granddaughter, the child clung desperately to her daddy's leg, peeking out with just one eye from where she had her head against his knee. I was sitting on a sofa between two of my sisters who look very much like me. I realized my granddaughter could not find me in that sea of faces. I leaned forward, held out my arms, smiled, and softly called her name.

It was one of those moments grandparents treasure. Her face lit up and like a shot she ran across the room and jumped into my lap. She nestled up against me and told me she was shy. I told her that was okay, and for a few minutes we talked quietly as I pointed out to her who all the people were. Gradually, her fear melted and she climbed down from my lap to join the other children playing on the floor.

I have no doubt that special moment would not have happened if I had not already established a relationship of love and trust with my granddaughter. She would not have been comfortable running to me in what was an overwhelming experience for her if she had not been accustomed to running to me in the good times. The same is true of our relationship with God — who is not only like a father to us, but also at times like a mother, or a loving grandparent. If we hope to confidently run to God with our fears and our sorrows, we must make a habit of turning to him in our everyday experiences and our joys. This is prayer — the building of a go-to relationship with God that will be an anchor for us in every situation.

As we seek to expand and enrich our prayer life, we may discover different ways to pray to God the Father, God the Son, or God the Holy Spirit. Different people develop different kinds of relationships with God and thus we all pray differently in the same way that we see the people in the Bible interacting differently with God.

For me, God the Father is the Creator, the giver of all the material gifts in my life. My prayers of praise and thanksgiving are often directed toward this awesome God. Jesus is human to me. He is my friend and also my healer. Just as he walked and talked with others, I can imagine him being present to me. I like to imagine being with him in the Gospel scenes, walking with him along the dusty roads, sitting next to him in the Temple, riding with him in a boat across the sea, kneeling beside him at Gethsemane. The Holy Spirit is the giver of spiritual gifts. I pray to this Third Person of the Trinity when I need inspiration, strength, guidance, courage, or faith. Just as I cannot see the Spirit, I cannot see the gifts he gives. Yet, through prayer, I know both are there.

Praying to three different Persons in one God might be a little confusing for our young grandchildren. We need to encourage them to pray in a way that is comforting and meaningful to them. Gradually we can introduce them to God as an awesome Father, a healing and forgiving Friend, or a mystical Spirit.

PLEASE GOD

My grandchildren were still asleep when I came to babysit. When the oldest one snuck down the stairs in the early morning light, she climbed into my lap for some snuggling.

"How are you?" I asked.

"Okay," she replied, "but I had a nightmare last night." She began to tell me the details of her dream. "Then I woke up," she said, "and I said, 'Please, God, let this be a bad dream.'" To demonstrate her point, she folded her little hands in the gesture she had used alone in the dark that night.

How often in our lives do we all whisper, "Please, God"? Please, God, let the medical tests come back good, let a relative find a job, let a marriage work out, let the chemo conquer the cancer. We are forever telling God what we want him to do. However, because God *is* God, he already knows what we want.

Thomas à Kempis, a medieval priest and author of the great spiritual classic *The Imitation of Christ*, includes in his book a wonderful prayer that puts our relationship with God in the right perspective. He says to God: "You know the future before it happens, and you do not need us to remind you of what is happening on earth. You know what I need for my spiritual progress…. You know me better and more clearly than anyone else. Grant me, Lord, to know what I ought to know, to love what I ought to love, to praise what is most pleasing to you, to esteem what seems most precious to you, to detest what is loathsome in your eyes."

If we can learn to put everything in God's hands the way Thomas à Kempis did, we can start using our time with God for more fulfilling and rewarding prayer than simply begging for favors. Praying for our needs and the needs of others is, of course, a good thing. But there is so much more to prayer than this. We may need to be reminded of that so we can teach our grandchildren prayer is not telling God what to do.

Yes, we can ask God for personal favors and for the needs of the world. He loves to answer those prayers for us. But we also need to take time to tell God how much we love him. We need to praise his goodness and the wonder and beauty of his creation. And we need to thank him for everything.

More importantly, we need to give God time to talk to us. It is important to realize God is not confined by the ten, twenty, or thirty minutes a day we might dedicate to him. God can respond to our prayers anytime, and in any way he chooses. That is part of being God. God can speak to us through the words of a friend, the lyrics of a song, the verses in Scripture, the beauty of nature, or the book that falls open to an inspiring or relevant page. We might begin the conversation with a morning prayer. But God will carry on the conversation with us throughout the day in ways we might find surprising and amazing.

BE STILL

Although God can speak to us in surprising ways, he often speaks to us in silence. When my granddaughter told me of her nightmare and her prayer to God, I asked her, "And did you hear God whisper, 'It's okay. It was just a dream'?" She looked at me for a minute confused and then slowly nodded that she had heard. I told her that sometimes when we are very, very quiet our hearts can hear God whisper to us.

But being still is not easy. This is a serious challenge, for even if we close our eyes and shut our mouths our minds are still firing endless thoughts and distractions at us. Our desire to hear God gets sidetracked as we mentally notice the spot on the floor, plan the grocery list, or replay a conversation we had with a coworker. Pushing aside this mental noise is an endless battle as we wait for God to speak. Yet we must be diligent for we know God comes in the quiet.

Mother Teresa, speaking once on the importance of silence in our prayer, said: "We cannot find God in noise or agitation. Nature: trees, flowers, and grass grow in silence. The stars, the moon and the sun move in silence." What a beautiful image she creates for us. Just being still with God. It is the best way to grow closer to him. Her message is not new. She is repeating what the prophet Elijah learned from God on a mountaintop thousands of years ago (see 1 Kgs 19:11–13).

Elijah waited for God to speak to him in a strong wind, an earthquake, and a fire. But God was not heard in any of these. It was only in the lightest whisper of a breeze that Elijah heard God. Like Elijah, we will not find God in the winds of our planning, the earthquakes of our disappointments, or the fires of our anger. When these thoughts are loud in our minds, it will be difficult to hear God. We must wait patiently for them to pass, for God speaks best to us in a small whisper.

Learning to be still is a skill that takes practice and experimentation. Some people can find the stillness they seek through meditation or centering prayer. Others may find that a special location will help quiet them — whether the back pew in an empty church, a bench overlooking a lake, or a rug in front of a fire. Hospital chapels are usually open twenty-four hours; I have found them to be a great place to find quiet.

HOW TO PRAY

When we were young, we may have learned certain ways to pray — a place to be, words to say, or gestures to make. These are only the tip of the beautiful iceberg that is prayer. There are so many wonderful ways to pray. We can pray through memorized prayers, journaling, song, or iPhone apps. We can dedicate our actions as prayer, or pray as we are going about our daily activities. The only rule with prayer is that we must do it. It is best if we can make a habit of praying at the same time every day. This way we do not forget. For many people, the best time to pray is first thing in the morning.

Saint Francis de Sales is often quoted as saying: "Every one of us needs half an hour of prayer each day, except when we are busy. Then we need an hour." A more modern version of this advice has shown up on the side of a coffee mug: "If you only pray when you are in trouble … you are in trouble." If we do not make prayer a habit in our lives, then prayer will be uncomfortable and awkward. And what could be worse than being uncomfortable with God?

Prayer does not even need to involve words. My youngest granddaughter was a quiet child. She did not cry much. If she wanted something, she would reach out both arms and with her hands face up she would begin rapidly opening and closing her little fists as if she were grabbing for something. It was almost impossible to deny those little raised hands reaching for the person or thing she wanted.

I imagine God looks down upon us just as fondly when we make gestures of prayer. It might be reverently bowing down on one knee before the tabernacle. It might be holding a rosary or crucifix while we cry. It might be making the Sign of the Cross before starting the car. It might be resting a hand on a favorite image of Our Lord, Our Lady, or a beloved saint. It might be lighting a candle in church or in our own homes. Or it might be simply reaching our hands out like a little child.

I was most aware of the many ways people pray when I appealed to friends and family for prayers for a very special intention. One sister gave up desserts as a prayer. Another sent a petition off to the Carmelite nuns. Some friends prayed the Divine Mercy Chaplet or the Rosary. One friend put my intention on her refrigerator where her whole family posted special prayer intentions. Various favorite saints were invoked by many people. I wrote intense letters to God in my prayer journal. I carried my plea, written on a slip of paper, with me all day. In the end, thousands of prayers were answered with good news. All was well.

Just as there are many ways to pray, we have endless opportunities to help our grandchildren get comfortable with prayer. We can encourage them to pray about things that worry them. We can ask them if they remembered to thank God for the blessings in their lives. We can introduce them to our favorite saints or our favorite prayer practices. If we don't have favorite saints and favorite prayers, now might be the time to seek out some that could be inspirational for our grandchildren as they grow into adulthood. We can also tell our grandchildren when we are praying for them. Telling them we are praying for them to have a good day or to do the right thing or to be safe on a field trip are ways to remind them of the constant blessings of praying.

For Reflection

1. Imagine talking with Jesus in a scene from one of the Gospels. This is a wonderful way to develop a closer prayer relationship with Jesus.

2. Does my prayer include too much time telling God what to do? What other conversations could I have with God besides just begging for favors?

3. Have I "heard" God speak to me through the people and things I encounter throughout my day? Am I open to hearing God in these ways?

4. When was the last time I tried a new form of prayer? Can I find one prayer practice to add to my life right now?

A Grandparent's Prayer

Dear God, I want to grow closer to you in prayer. Please show me the way. Let my prayer life be a good witness to my grandchildren so they will never be afraid to run to you in their joys and in their sorrows, in their needs and in their gratitude. Give me time to be still with you throughout this day and every day of my life. Help me to hear your gentle whisper throughout my day. Give me the grace to go where you call me. Amen.

Chapter 16

Gratitude

"I want you all to make a picture," my friend said as she passed out paper and art supplies to her many grandchildren ranging in ages from toddler to teen. My friend had gathered her flock of grandchildren onto a hillside of a place they called "the farm." It was a lovely piece of rural property, which had been passed down for generations. On weekends, her children and grandchildren often gathered there to get away from the city, enjoy the beauty of nature, and have some simple outdoor fun together.

My friend had decided she wanted her grandchildren to stop on this beautiful fall day and really take time to appreciate the gift of this country place. She asked them each to make a picture of what they treasured most about this place they often took for granted. The pictures, she told me, were amazing. She was impressed by how willingly they undertook the task and how creative their expressions of appreciation were.

Sadly, in today's world, we don't take enough time to appreciate the beautiful gifts God has given us. In no other time of history have we been so aware of what we do *not* have. Advertising and tweets from friends constantly remind us of what we have not yet bought or experienced. We spend so much time longing for the new and different. We forget to be grateful for the here and now, the good and the comfortable. In the last of his three rules for life, Saint Paul tells us, "In all circumstances, give thanks" (1 Thes 5:18). Yet how often do we stop and give thanks? More importantly, how well are we calling our grandchildren to take time to express their gratitude?

Meister Eckhart, a Dominican preacher, philosopher, and theologian is often quoted as saying, "If the only prayer you ever say in your entire life is 'thank you,' it is enough." Gratitude is a necessary key to a healthy spiritual life and a foundational virtue for a good life. But gratitude is a virtue seriously missing in our lives today. Let us show our grandchildren how to be grateful.

BEING HUMBLE

First, however, we must be humble. Humility is another virtue not highly valued these days. We often think of the humble person as the doormat who cannot stand up for himself or herself. Nothing could be further from the truth. Many strong, successful, and powerful people are humble. Humility basically means recognizing the reality of Saint Paul's words to the Corinthians: "What do you possess that you have not received? But if you have received it, why are you boasting as if you did not receive it?" (1 Cor 4:7).

Absolutely everything we have is a gift from God. God sent us to this earth with a prepackaged set of skills, talents, and attributes which would allow us to do something unique, something no one else would do. God placed us in a family that could supply us with the opportunities and/or challenges that would be most important to us. Our education, health, experiences, and the endless other circumstances of our lives have all played key roles in making us the people we are today — the people God made us to be. Even the drive, resourcefulness, and determination which may have gotten us through tough spots are gifts from God. We can take credit for absolutely nothing! Each one of us is a child of God — uniquely formed by him alone.

Once we humbly realize everything we have is a gift, we can start being truly grateful. When we say "thank you" to someone, we acknowledge we could not have done it on our own. And none of us could have taken our first breath or made it where we are in life today without God's divine help and without the help of countless people who have touched our lives in both huge and small ways.

As my grandchildren became older, they would often tell me, "I can do it myself, Grandma." We may try to say the same thing to God, even when nothing is further from the truth. Yet realizing we need help can be difficult in a world which teaches us to be independent. As the oldest child of six, I heard, more often, "You don't need help," rather than, "Would you like help?" As a result, I came to see wanting or needing help as a weakness and an inconvenience to those around me. Many of us may have learned the same lesson growing up. Now we need to unlearn it and be able to admit that, yes, we do need help. And we need to be grateful for the help we receive from God and from others. If we cannot accept and admit our own helplessness, it is unlikely that we will know true gratitude.

We do not go through a day without assistance from other people. Those close to us help us with our daily living. Those who are distant strangers grow the food we eat, construct the highways we drive upon, and maintain the energy sources that power our lives. Let us begin to humbly pay attention to the ways countless people help us throughout our lives.

ACTIVELY GRATEFUL

It was a beautiful fall day when my daughter and I took my grandchildren to a local family attraction. We had a wonderful time feeding goats and camels, watching an elephant show, riding the carousel, getting little faces painted, and having some special snacks. As we were waiting for the tram to take us back to the parking lot, my granddaughter picked up a spectacular red leaf. "Grandma, isn't this pretty?" she asked.

"Oh, it is beautiful," I exclaimed. "I love the red leaves the best."

She smiled and handed it to me. "You can have it, Grandma," she said, "because you took us to this fun place."

Not to be outdone, my grandson quickly scurried to find an equally beautiful leaf to present to me as a thank-you gift. Those leaves — along with pictures from the day — are preserved in a frame which sits in my entry hall. For me, they are a reminder of my grandchildren's active gratitude.

True gratitude must be active. We can say we are grateful, but unless we do something to show that gratitude, our words can seem empty and meaningless. Consider the story of the ten lepers cured by Jesus (see Lk 17:11–19).

Remember the story? Ten lepers are cured. Only one returned to give thanks. Does that mean the other ones were not grateful? I doubt it. Surely, they were partying with their friends saying, "Thank God I am free of that disease!" But only one did something about his feeling of gratitude. Only one went back to find Jesus. He was actively grateful!

We may want to believe we are like the one who went back to Jesus. But we may be more like the nine lepers who were so busy celebrating their good fortune that they never showed their gratitude in a positive way. How can we actively show our gratitude for the blessings we have received? The most meaningful way might be to pay it forward.

"Pay it forward" means to show gratitude for something good someone did for us by doing something good for someone else. We are called to pay it forward for every single blessing God has given us. Yes, we should say prayers of praise and thanksgiving to God. But that is not the only or best way to show appreciation to a God who repeatedly asks us to care for the needy, welcome the stranger, and comfort the sorrowing. True gratitude calls us to do more than just voice our appreciation. It calls us to go out and do something good for someone else.

When an angel appears in Scripture, we better believe this heavenly being is bringing a very important message. The Archangel Raphael delivered such a message to Tobit and Tobias in the Old Testament. Raphael, disguised as a man, had accompanied Tobit's son Tobias on an important, yet dangerous, journey. When Tobias returned safely, he wanted to pay Raphael for his help. At that point Raphael revealed himself as an angel and gave an important two-part message to all mankind about how we should repay the goodness of God: "Bless God and give him thanks before all the living for the good things he has done for you, by blessing and extolling his name in song. Proclaim before all with due honor the deeds of

God, and do not be slack in thanking him.... Do good, and evil will not overtake you.... It is better to give alms than to store up gold, for almsgiving saves from death, and purges all sin. Those who give alms will enjoy a full life" (Tb 12:6–9). Praise God and give to those in need. This is how we are told to be actively grateful.

When we are truly grateful, we realize we have more than enough to share. In appreciation for all the good things in our lives we are ready to open our hearts, our homes, and our wallets to those in need.

BEING AWARE

It is difficult to be properly grateful if we are not aware of all the good in our lives. We can practice gratitude by humbly becoming more conscious of how other people help us through the day. Do we thank them? Let our grandchildren see us saying a sincere thank-you to the person who bagged our groceries, the man who delivered the package at our door, or the woman who served us at a restaurant. Every day brings endless opportunities for us to recognize the contributions other people make to our lives. Yet we often overlook them.

Just as we may not acknowledge or appreciate the good things other people do for us, we often fail to acknowledge and appreciate God's endless blessings. How often do we stop and say, "Thank you, God!" to the One who gives us every precious detail of every moment we live?

We can expand our practice of gratitude by setting aside time in our day to be intentionally aware of and grateful for the gifts each day brings. For five or ten minutes, we can just sit quietly and do a gratitude meditation. Breathe in, saying, "thank you." Then breathe out, saying, "for," and then name the first thing that comes to mind. It might surprise you what amazing things you have to be thankful for in an ordinary day.

Another intentional practice to make us more aware of our need to be grateful is to make notes in a gratitude journal. Before going to bed we can write a quick thank-you note to God for the blessings of that day. If we date the entries, we can go back and remind ourselves of the blessings from a week, a month, or a year ago. If we are too tired to write before bed, we can use the beads of our rosary to count off ten blessings of the day before drifting off to sleep. When we consciously strive to become more aware of the gifts in our lives, we soon realize how much we owe back to God.

To set our grandchildren on the path of thankfulness, we should make a point of regularly thanking them for the little things they do so they realize how good it feels to be thanked. One way to do this is to display and use the gifts they give us. I have a red paper fox with a brown pompom nose on my refrigerator, which my granddaughter made for me two years ago. She was so proud of that gift. To this day, she often smiles and says, "You still have the fox I made you in preschool." And I tell her I am still happy she gave it to me.

Sadly, our world is slowly forgetting the art of giving thanks. Sabbath was originally set aside as a time to give thanks. It was a time for us to sit back, just as God did on the seventh day, and see that our lives are good. When we never stop being busy, we never have time to realize how blessed we are. Sabbath, or Sunday, can be a time for us to spend with God and with family. The word *eucharist*, which was always the traditional way for a family to celebrate Sunday, comes from the Greek word for gratitude. Yet, today, many families do not celebrate a weekly day of rest, thanksgiving, or *eucharist*.

We are also losing our annual day for gratitude — Thanksgiving Day. Year after year, giving thanks is being replaced by wanting more. Black Friday has become a more important day in many homes than Thanksgiving. Our traditional annual day for remembering our blessings is being interrupted by parents and teens having to rush off to retail jobs and frantic buyers more interested in using the dining-room table for comparing ads rather than sharing a meal with loved ones. As much as possible, let us truly celebrate Sabbath and Thanksgiving in our homes. It will bring us joy.

The simple reality is that a grateful person is a joyful person. Pope Francis tells us: "To be able to offer thanks, to be able to praise the Lord for what he has done for us: this is important!... Only those who know how to say 'Thank you' will experience the fullness of joy."

BLESSED ARE WE

The first time I went to celebrate Grandparents Day at my granddaughter's preschool, the children were required to introduce their grandparents. The teacher then made a nametag for us, using the name the child had said. My granddaughter identified me as "Grandma Sue." It is one of my most treasured nametags. I have spoken at conferences around the country and have received name badges with lots of added ribbons and titles upon them, but no nametag is more special than the one that says, "Grandma Sue." I am most grateful for this phase of my life.

As we become older, and hopefully wiser, we begin to realize what truly matters in this life and what does not. When our grandchildren come crying to us because they could not get the toy or the adventure they wanted, we, in our wisdom, know none of this will matter in just a few years (or minutes!). The simplest things are usually the memories and blessings we cherish the most.

It is the greatest of gifts to be able to wake every morning and think, "How blessed I am!" or, "My life is perfect just the way it is." If we pass this ability to be grateful for the present moment to our grandchildren, we will be giving them a treasure they will remember for years — a treasure more valuable than the latest character T-shirt or newest electronic toy.

It is said the grateful heart wants for nothing. It is impossible to be truly grateful and discontent at the same time. When we live life with gratitude, we spend more time counting our blessings than whining about our wants. We find joy in what we have. We do not have the worries and burdens of too many possessions and too many expectations.

If we spend time comparing our lives to those who have more than we do, we can become envious. But, when we look at people who have less than we do, we can become grateful. It is all a matter of where we train our eyes and thoughts. Do we count our blessings or dream of our wants?

To realize how blessed we are, it is helpful to expose ourselves and our grandchildren to those who are poor throughout the world. We must not turn away. Modern media tends to expose us to those who have all kinds of fine things. When we watch most television shows or movies, we walk away wanting more — bigger homes, nicer clothes, newer cars. When we educate ourselves about the poor of the world, we begin to realize how much God has already blessed us. Looking into the faces of people who are poor may make us uncomfortable, but it can also make us grateful instead of envious, generous instead of self-serving. We see God has already given us all we need, plus enough to share with others.

One way to encourage grandchildren to see their lives as good is to ask them what was best about their day, their week, or the outing we just completed with them. By teaching them to focus on the good, we teach them to be grateful. When we are doing chores with our grandkids, we can distract them from the work by talking about the fun they had making the mess — whether it was building with blocks or baking in the kitchen. When we complete a jigsaw puzzle, we can pause to tell each other what is our favorite part of the picture. Learning to see the good is a step toward learning to be grateful.

Rather than trying to shower our grandchildren with great gifts, let us show them how to be grateful for small blessings. When we teach them this lesson, we prepare them for a life of contentment and happiness.

For Reflection

1. Am I humble enough to realize it is help from God and from others which has brought me to where I am today?

2. How have I been actively grateful in the past? How could I actively show my gratitude right now for the blessing of my grandchildren in my life?

3. Do I spend some time on a regular basis being grateful for the blessings of my life?

4. What might be a way I could help my grandchildren grow up feeling more grateful and less envious or entitled?

A Grandparent's Prayer

Great Spirit of Goodness and Love, please be with me always to remind me of all that is good in my life. Help me to be a more humble and grateful person. Give me a little nudge when you present me with opportunities to express my gratitude to you by doing something good for someone else. Let me share my gratitude with my grandchildren, so they grow to know you are all good and their lives are greatly blessed. Thank you for everything! Amen.

FINAL THOUGHT

I encountered two adult grandchildren recently at a funeral for a ninety-four-year-old man. The first was a young mother who was waiting for her grandmother outside the funeral home. The older woman no longer drove, so in the middle of a busy weekend this young woman had taken her grandmother to pay her last respects to a dear friend.

As the grandmother was being helped into the car she reached up and patted her granddaughter's cheek. "I do not know what I would do without her," the grandmother told me.

The granddaughter smiled and replied, "I do not know what I would do without her."

The next morning at the funeral, the oldest grandson of the deceased man gave a eulogy. He stated very simply: "I am the man I am today, in part, because of my grandpa. He taught me so many important values. I try to live like him every day of my life."

Wouldn't it be the greatest blessing if each of us could have grandchildren like these two? Grandchildren who love us, care for us, and feel we have helped make them better people. By living and sharing the virtues discussed in this book we just might be able to make that happen. May God bless each and all of us on that journey.